BEYOND BANNED BOOKS

ALA Editions purchases fund advocacy, awareness, and accreditation programs for library professionals worldwide.

BEYOND BANNED BOOKS

Defending Intellectual Freedom throughout Your Library

KRISTIN PEKOLL

ALA Office for
Intellectual Freedom

CHICAGO | 2019

Kristin Pekoll is assistant director of the American Library Association's Office for Intellectual Freedom in Chicago. For twelve years she was the youth librarian at the West Bend Community Memorial Library in Wisconsin. Her primary focus is supporting librarians who are dealing with censorship issues, and she also works to raise awareness of the value of intellectual freedom within the library profession and among the public.

© 2019 by the American Library Association

Extensive effort has gone into ensuring the reliability of the information in this book; however, the publisher makes no warranty, express or implied, with respect to the material contained herein.

ISBNs
978-0-8389-1901-9 (paper)
978-0-8389-1890-6 (PDF)
978-0-8389-1889-0 (ePub)
978-0-8389-1891-3 (Kindle)

Library of Congress Cataloging-in-Publication Data
Names: Pekoll, Kristin, author. | American Library Association. Office for Intellectual Freedom.
Title: Beyond banned books : defending intellectual freedom throughout your library / Kristin Pekoll.
Description: Chicago : ALA Editions, 2019. | Includes index. | Includes bibliographical references and index.
Identifiers: LCCN 2018059726 | ISBN 9780838919019 (pbk. : alk. paper) | ISBN 9780838918890 (epub) | ISBN 9780838918906 (pdf) | ISBN 9780838918913 (kindle)
Subjects: LCSH: Libraries—Censorship—United States. | Libraries—Censorship—United States—Case studies. | Intellectual freedom—United States. | Librarians—Professional ethics—United States.
Classification: LCC Z711.4 .P38 2019 | DDC 025.2/13—dc23
LC record available at https://lccn.loc.gov/2018059726

Book design by Kim Thornton in the Charis and Intro typefaces. Cover image © mrhighsky/Adobe Stock

⊚ This paper meets the requirements of ANSI/NISO Z39.48–1992 (Permanence of Paper).

Printed in the United States of America

23 22 21 20 19   5 4 3 2 1

CONTENTS

Foreword, by Martin Garnar vii
Preface: "You're Going to Hell" ix
Introduction: Pushing the Needle xiii

1 Displays and Exhibits — 1

2 Artwork — 13

3 Programs and Events — 29

4 Bookmarks and Reading Lists — 45

5 Social Media — 61

6 Databases — 77

7 Report and Support — 89

Appendix

The Library Bill of Rights 99
Access to Digital Information, Services, and Networks 101
Access to Library Resources and Services Regardless of Sex,
Gender Identity, Gender Expression, or Sexual Orientation 106
Challenged Resources 109
Education and Information Literacy 112
Equity, Diversity, Inclusion 115
Exhibit Spaces and Bulletin Boards 120
Library-Initiated Programs as a Resource 122
Politics in American Libraries 125
The Universal Right to Free Expression 128
Visual and Performing Arts in Libraries 132
Code of Ethics 136

Index 139

FOREWORD

Martin Garnar
Dean of the Kraemer Family Library
University of Colorado Colorado Springs

HEN WE talk about censorship with people who don't work in libraries, it's pretty clear that Banned Books Week has turned into one of our profession's most successful marketing campaigns. People will stop me and talk about their favorite banned books, and how it made them feel like a rebel to read something that bothered someone else. At my academic library, students are incensed each year by our display of challenged books, since they cannot fathom why anyone would want to take a book off the shelf just because they don't agree with it.

"Just don't read it if you don't like it!"
"How can people be so ignorant?"
"No one should ever ban a book."

Banned Books Week itself can become the target of complaints. At my previous institution, a faculty member complained about our library's Banned Books Week display, contending that we were misleading our users by suggesting that all of the books in the display had been banned, when some had "merely" been challenged. In response, a staff member changed the sign from "Banned Books" to "Controversial Titles" without consulting the display's creators. Since no books were removed from the display and the display was not taken down, maybe you think it's a stretch to call this censorship, but I would argue that altering content because it makes someone uncomfortable or angry is leading you down that road.

When the conversation moves beyond books, the same people who will defend Harry Potter or their favorite graphic novel to their dying day don't seem to have a problem when a school district removes students' access to an entire suite of databases because of spurious complaints about pornography by one set of parents.

> "There are some limits to what we should allow in schools."
>
> "It's a shame, but they can just get the information from somewhere else."

These are quotes from a conversation I had about the wholesale removal of one vendor's databases from over 100 schools in my home state of Colorado. Who was I talking with? Someone who works with libraries.

Censorship is no longer just for books, nor has it been for quite a while. In these contentious times, free and unfettered access to information is more important than ever, and this book is coming out when we are at a professional crossroads: how to support intellectual freedom and equity, diversity, and inclusion all at the same time. The difficult process of updating the American Library Association's policy guidelines for library meeting rooms has highlighted the divide between those who feel there must be appropriate limits on who can use them (i.e., no Nazis) and those who see any limits as a slippery slope (i.e., "everyone" means everyone, even if they ultimately mean us harm). While this book can't bridge a decades-old divide, it does give us plenty to consider as Kristin Pekoll examines the many ways that access to information—especially of underrepresented perspectives—is being restricted beyond the banning of books.

PREFACE
"You're Going to Hell!"

**OT YOU;** they were talking to me. That was the message left for me on a voicemail ten years ago. Librarians rarely choose their career path with a desire to occupy the spotlight or be in the center of a controversy. I know I didn't. I knew at the age of fourteen that I wanted to be a librarian and that I believed in this profession and its values. I wanted to work with smart people, kind people, open-minded people. I wanted to work with young people and steer them towards a bigger, brighter, bolder future. I'm not a shy person or a conservative person, but I never imagined that I would become known (falsely) as a porn purveyor with a gay agenda, or that I would be told I was going to hell and I shouldn't be around children. As distressing as these opinions were while I was in the midst of the situation, my values of intellectual freedom never wavered, which only reinforced the certainty that I had chosen my profession correctly.

In February 2009, I was the young adult librarian at the West Bend Community Memorial Library in Wisconsin. I had started working there while finishing my MLIS degree at the University of Wisconsin – Milwaukee in 2003. I loved working with teen volunteers and ordering young adult (YA) materials and growing as a young librarian. Posting booklists on library websites was a newer thing at the time, and I had just taken over the management of the website. I had no idea that one booklist would lead to a book challenge case targeting over eighty LGBTQ books; those five months defined my career, and they are the reason why I work for the Office for Intellectual Freedom and the reason I wrote this book.

I close my eyes today and I can instantly remember sitting in my car in the library parking lot sobbing. The pounding thought in my head was "I just want this to be over" again and again and again. I remember the fear every time I saw I had a new voicemail message. I remember sitting across from the parents who were so upset about these LGBTQ books, while I was armed with as many sources as I could get to defend these books and the teens who read them. I started shaking during that meeting as they read out loud a scene from *The Perks of Being a Wallflower* by Stephen Chbosky. All my defenses were torn to shreds, when a parent glared at me and demanded to know if I was a mother. She said that I couldn't be a mother because no mother would promote this pornography. It took everything I had not to protectively cover the baby inside me.

I would call my mom. I would talk to my colleagues. I would vent to my husband. But it wasn't until I spoke with Angela Maycock at the ALA's Office for Intellectual Freedom (OIF) that I felt someone understood the stress of the situation and completely validated my struggles. She made me laugh when things were anything but funny, and she reminded me how important these books were, especially in a community that claimed that "we don't have any gay kids here." I'm lucky and thankful to still be friends with Angela.

During the days of the challenge, while working at the library, I would put on my bravest face, even though I often felt I had no idea what I was doing. Now that I'm working in the same office that Angela Maycock once worked in, I realize that my experience is an incredibly common one for librarians who are going through a book challenge. Even the most seasoned librarians say they feel like they are being hit by a Mack truck or are staggering blind down a deserted street. Because you can read every book on intellectual freedom and book censorship; you can attend every webinar and conference session; you can memorize the website—but when a challenge happens to you, you still feel attacked, alone, and uncertain. Because every single intellectual freedom case is unique. You never know when it's going to happen. You never know who is going to be offended or why. And nowadays, you don't even know if it's going to be about a book. The challenge could be about a display or an artwork in the library, or about a library's social media post, or even about a database to which students have access in a school district.

With this book, I wanted to provide a resource that would help librarians when challenges arise that don't fit the traditional mold of *books*. Instead, they involve other media and formats. These challenges can involve artworks, displays and exhibits, programs, readers' advisory services and booklists, social media, and even databases. I wanted to showcase these types of challenges because they are often misunderstood and underreported and it helps librarians appreciate the broad spectrum of resources they provide and the value they hold to the institution. We have to know about these challenges in order to uncover the resources that are needed to support the librarians confronted by those challenges. We can't fix a problem we don't know about.

I am in a unique position to see every challenge that is reported to the American Library Association. Not only do I see the reports, but I talk to the librarians involved in responding to the challenges, and I chronicle the details. When we, my colleagues and I at the Office for Intellectual Freedom, take a step back every year and look at the larger trends and issues that are surfacing, we see an increase in the challenges to library displays, to programs, and to reading lists. We see that social media posts are deleted because of their alleged racial bias, and pages are removed from books because of alleged political bias. We see a country where a president issues a cease-and-desist letter to a publisher of an upcoming book because the president doesn't like how he is portrayed in it. We see challenges of every type, in every kind of library, for every reason and by every kind of initiator.

I am awed and inspired by the librarians, educators, and activists who are refusing to sit quietly while their rights are challenged and denied and they themselves are personally threatened and abused. It's important to me that I do what I can in supporting the push for equitable access, inclusive learning environments, and diverse voices in publishing and in education. I recognize my privilege of being a straight white woman in a field that is dominated by straight white women. I'm privileged to be able to publish this book, and if it can push the needle towards what is right and just and kind in this world, and if it can support and encourage librarians in their careers, I will consider the book successful.

In my work and in my writing, I often think gratefully of Michael Tyree and the West Bend community who walked alongside me during the challenge and remain my friends wherever life takes us. I thank Barbara Jones and the Office for Intellectual Freedom for taking a chance on this Wisconsinite and giving me a home within the American Library Association. I am beholden to my family: my parents, Scott and Lynn, who have supported and loved me every day of my life; my kids, Joey and Annie, who give me hope for the future; and my husband, James, who holds us all together. And I am especially beholden to my mentor, Jamie LaRue; I am inspired by your peace and strength in the face of criticism, which has shown me that what people say does not make you who you are. Thank you for believing in me.

And finally, to internet trolls and book censors around the world and in my backyard, you know who you are—and thank you, for without you, none of this would have ever been possible. Through your challenges and criticisms I have learned the strength of my own convictions and my character.

INTRODUCTION
Pushing the Needle

EADERS WILL notice a common theme throughout the examples of censorship (both attempted ones and successful ones) in this book. The majority of the resources, displays, and programs discussed in this book give a voice to historically marginalized perspectives or underrepresented people. People resist what they don't understand. They challenge the different, the unknown. In contrast, libraries are embracing the unknown. Librarians are looking for new ideas, different perspectives, broader language, and more diverse identities.

In approaching the world with open arms, librarians and educators have often encountered walls. Walls that stand against justice, equality, and kindness. Sometimes those walls are laid with internal bricks. These internal bricks may look like biased library policies or unequal permissions. As we uncover these walls in our institutions, we start conversations. Discussions and debates have grown about library neutrality and systemic racism and hate speech. Sometimes those walls are built by external hands using the weapons of hate and fear. Situations are reported about public institutions encountering hate-filled graffiti or legislation that denies access and civil liberties to our patrons. Many librarians in our profession believe that we can't overcome the rift between the values of free speech on the one hand, and of furthering social justice on the other; that we can't conquer the walls. But

I'm a firm believer that we can support both principles. Martin Garnar wrote a response about how to overcome this rift in *Library Journal:*

> We continue to support free speech and fight the laws that target marginalized communities. We continue to confront and dismantle the structural inequality in our profession and our society, and continue to work with marginalized communities to improve their access to information. And we continue to have thoughtful discussions about how to make this a "both and" situation as opposed to "either or."[1]

This book will push against the walls and encourage conversations on how we can preserve the pluralistic values of our profession by defending intellectual freedom.

Libraries are no longer solely repositories for the information that has traditionally been published in books. Libraries' missions aren't just about books anymore. Yes, libraries still collect and circulate books in fulfillment of their mission, but that mission is so much broader now. Librarians are providing education and access to information in many different formats and technologies now. Today's librarians understand the much larger role of libraries in their community. That role involves much more than just literacy. It is about lifelong learning, community-building, and affirmations of identity. The library is the one place left in our culture where all people are welcome to loiter, to browse, to explore, and to be with no ulterior motive or agenda.

Librarians engage their communities on a much larger scale than ever before. The professional resources and published trade books about displays, programs, readers' advisory services, and social media have skyrocketed. Facebook and Pinterest are excellent sources for unlimited, creative, and engaging ideas. Librarians are providing education and access to information in different formats and technologies. Generations of librarians now and in the future are trained in marketing, outreach, and programs in addition to reference, collection development, and cataloging. But no one discusses the liability involved with creating or showcasing content that is affiliated with a public institution. We create this content with no sense of structure or responsibility, and this leaves our information experts vulnerable to crashing into the walls of challenges and censorship.

The core of our professional values embraces equitable access to information for all, including many underserved populations. To provide truly equitable access, we need to also provide equitable representation of all points of view in all types of content. Gaining awareness of inequality in these populations leads many professionals to advance social justice within their institutions. We do this by creating book displays about the Black Lives Matter movement or LGBT History Month, or other potentially controversial issues. We invite controversial speakers or host progressive programs. But creating content within a public institution can open our administration to complaints from those who may possess a different viewpoint. And while the profession is well-versed in protecting the right to read books, many libraries lack the policies and experience needed to address the creation of the content provided by you—the staff.

Defending and advocating for the rights of others is easier than defending and advocating for our own rights. We librarians have the right and obligation to use all of the professional development skills and talent that we have acquired in the work we do. I wish there was a verb, like teach, that describes what we do—to *library*. We seek. We know. We promote. We provide. We engage. We teach. We learn. We develop. We lead. We create. We think. We guide. We train. We defend. There is no verb that fully encapsulates all that we do. And because we can't fully define what we do, it is difficult to defend it. Readers have the right to read. Writers have the right to speak. Teachers have the right to teach. But where is the right to be a librarian outlined?

There is so much passion and knowledge in our colleagues. In order to nourish that passion in our profession, we need to support one another and the work that we do. And not just support the status quo, but support our skills and knowledge, especially when we "push the needle" towards equity, diversity, inclusion, and intellectual freedom.

This book provides many vivid examples of the censorship of resources and services beyond challenged and banned books. Each chapter addresses a different resource or service.

- Each chapter begins with a description of how the resource or service is created, and the civil and intellectual liberties that are assumed when creating that content.
- The next section discusses recent public situations that exemplify the possible complaints and controversies involving that resource or service. These situations primarily involve public institutions (libraries, schools, universities, or government agencies) located within the United States.

- Following these specific case studies, I draw connections between the legal and constitutional defenses implicit in the skills of our profession. When possible I try to include relevant opinions by our country's courts. I am not an attorney and do not have a law degree, so the information included here should not be considered legal advice.
- I highlight the importance of preparation with sample policies and relevant professional resources, many of which have been adopted by the ALA Council. I often include practical guidance and questions to consider when strengthening your library's defenses against censorship.

Many of the case studies discussed in this book are drawn from my work as the assistant director of the Office for Intellectual Freedom and from my personal interactions with librarians on the front line. Hundreds of librarians contact the office every year to either report challenges or look for guidance and support (or both). I am usually their first contact. Having gone through a challenge myself, I have firsthand understanding of the need for this book and for practical support resources. While we know that we don't hear all the stories and challenges encountered, we hear enough of them to know that help is needed.

While many of the case studies that I include in this book to demonstrate the widening problem of censorship are public stories that were chronicled in newspapers and publications, occasionally I reference a situation that was shared to me without journalistic validation. I hope you can trust my integrity to relay the story that fits within these chapters without betraying a colleague's confidence.

Final Note

I've had the pleasure and honor of working with two exceptional directors at the Office for Intellectual Freedom: Jamie LaRue and Barbara Jones. But I will always feel a little sad that I never got to meet the powerhouse, Judith Krug.

Stories still circulate within the ALA about Judith Krug's passion and tenacity. She was known to be a First Amendment purist, and she was uncompromising in her support of librarians and the freedom to read. But there is one story about Judith that has always stuck with me because of how contrary it runs to her character. In a confidential conversation with a librarian about a book being pulled from the library shelf without following policy, Judith was heard consoling the woman gently and reassuring her. When faced with the personal decision to stand against censorship or remain silent, Judith—strong, powerful, vocal Judith—counseled that sometimes it's better to push the needle towards intellectual freedom only quietly, and thereby keep your job, rather than slam the truth over their heads and end up out of a job.

I understand how strong our desire is to right the injustices of our society. I encourage you to be thoughtful about when and how we act. We can do more from inside the profession and the library institution than we can ever do on the outside. Hopefully, this book will aid you as you continue to protect diverse voices from censorship and build more inclusive libraries that represent and welcome all people and ideas.

NOTE

1. Kara Yorio and Lisa Peet, "Free Speech Debate Erupts with ALA's Inclusion of Hate Groups in Revision of Bill of Rights Interpretation," *School Library Journal,* July 10, 2018, https://www.slj.com/?detailStory=free-speech-debate-erupts-alas-inclusion-hate-groups-bill-rights-revision.

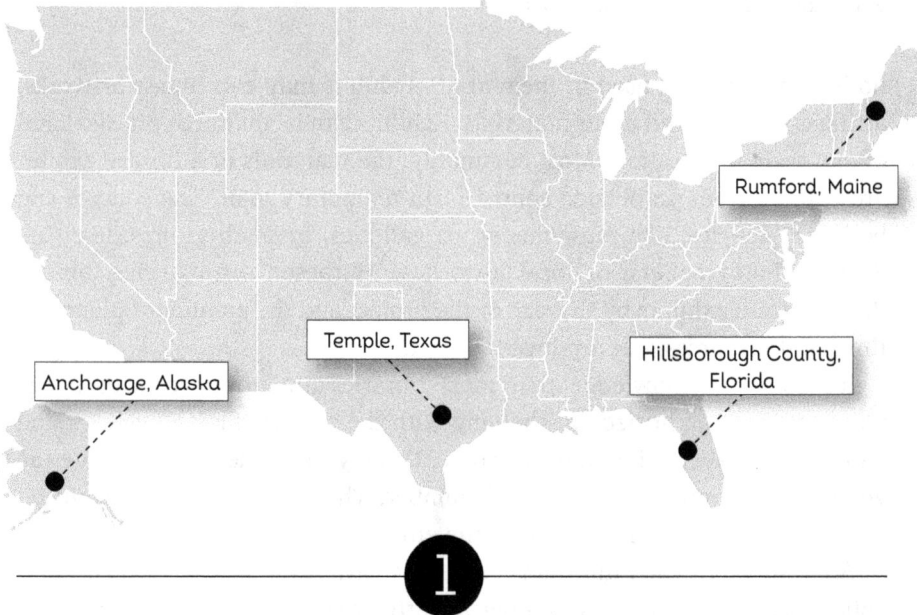

1

Displays and Exhibits

"DESIGN CREATES CULTURE. CULTURE SHAPES VALUES. VALUES determine the future." This quote from the world-renowned designer and educator Robert L. Peters connects visual design with active verbs about how the world is perceived. Libraries, too, use visual design in displays and exhibits in order to connect users with information possibilities.

Free-Range Browsing

The term *display* is often used casually by library staff to describe the placement of materials with the covers facing out to attract attention. The most common type of display in libraries is a book display. In *Creative Management of Small Public Libraries in the 21st Century,* author Cynthia Harbeson writes about the need for small libraries to establish their space as a community center through the intentional use of inviting displays and physical spaces that are welcoming and engaging.[1] She establishes a working definition for library displays by adapting the dictionary definition to the library environment: a display is "any creative arrangement of objects on view for a specific purpose." A cousin of the display is the library exhibit. Exhibits are usually broader in their sources and materials than displays are. Exhibits often include more than a library's internal collections, and in fact, sometimes

1

no library items are used in them at all. Exhibits may encompass artworks, artifacts, objects, and other materials. Exhibits can be online or physical and of any scale or duration. Most commonly, the materials in a library exhibit are curated from an outside source for a temporary loan. The sources can be large agencies, like museums or art galleries, or small groups, like Cub Scouts, photographers, or local historians. Harbeson distinguishes library displays from exhibits by the size of the project and the amount of planning, time, and resources that are invested in it.

It's common knowledge that most libraries are arranged with books placed upright on horizontal shelving with their spines facing outward and a directional label adhered to the spine. Usually the spine labels include the general collection area with a call number. These materials are organized systematically for retrieval and for the efficient use of space.

Alternatively, when librarians create displays from the materials in their collections, the intention is to showcase attractive book covers and highlight relevant topics or new materials. Displays differ from traditional organization by disregarding call numbers, collections, formats, and uniformity. Displays allow librarians to embrace their inner creative artist.

Displays have a multitude of purposes. They are attractive and eye-catching, and they often welcome and entice users into the space. Displays showcase materials that might otherwise get overlooked. Displays increase foot traffic to different areas within the building. Displays offer opportunities to cross-promote additional services and events in the library.

The market for display furniture, shelving, easels, signage, and accessories has grown exponentially in the last few decades. The funding available for creating displays has also increased. Terms like *visual merchandising* have spread beyond the retail industry to the information profession. Searching Pinterest, blogs, and social media for ideas for new displays can often stimulate a librarian's creativity. The range of complexity, skill, quality, and size of material displays can vary greatly. These variables may depend on the staff that libraries have available to devote to the projects, or they may simply depend on what space is available. Many newer libraries have prioritized display space with their designers and architects. By contrast, some rural or small neighborhood libraries are lucky if they can find display space along the top of a high bookshelf against a wall.

The libraries with the most successful displays mirror the practices and strategies of bookstores and other retailers. When priority is given to attracting customers and is shifted away from simply stocking inventory, the circulation of library materials skyrockets. In a culture of selling and advertising, visual appeal and catching the attention of the audience are as important for the Boise Public Library as they are for Barnes & Noble.

Some libraries don't understand the value of high-quality displays. After all, it can be difficult to measure the success of a display. Library managers need to balance the time spent to create and maintain displays with the fuzzy output of their value. Often, the needs of performing other tasks are more pressing than that of creating a display. Similarly, if a library doesn't value the resource, there is less intentional thought about how displays are created, who is responsible for them, and what the parameters are for displaying the materials in them. Librarians consider displays a valuable commodity, yet rarely is this professional function considered in job descriptions, budgets, training, or education.

What is lacking in most of our profession's literature, either formal or casual, are guidelines about the subject content of library displays. Obvious display ideas include readers' advisory requests that often get asked, such as "If you like James Patterson, try one of these books," or "Binge-worthy reads for fans of *Stranger Things*." There are also upcoming program cross-promotions such as "Impress our visiting magician with card tricks and laugh-out-loud jokes," or "Familiarize yourself with canning and food preservation in anticipation of our master gardener program." Displays often showcase specific formats like audiobooks, large-print materials, or graphic novels. These all seem like innocent display ideas, right?

Concerns and complaints can arise from even the best and most innocent of intentions, however. A display about *Stranger Things* might include Stephen King's horror novel *It*, which has historically been frequently challenged. It could include *Paper Girls*, by Brian K. Vaughan, whose artistic work on the graphic novel, *Saga* was included in ALA's Top Ten Most Challenged Books of 2014. Additionally, critics of graphic novels have often stated that the books are lowbrow and pornographic.

Libraries will often use displays to recognize significant or historical events. There are weeks and months that pay homage to underrepresented populations, such as Black History Month or GLBT Book Month. Librarians are connecting recent events with calendar celebrations to create displays that draw attention to stories and viewpoints that are neglected, or to highlight their library's mission of inclusivity. They are spotlighting Martin Luther King Jr.'s birthday in January with materials about the Black Lives Matter movement.

No act in the library is too small to foster tolerance and acceptance. Many librarians are embracing their roles as display designers in order to highlight resources and themes in their collections on relevant issues in the news and on people who are change-makers.[2]

Meg, from a public library in Connecticut, created a display in the children's room around a quote from Mr. Rogers that says, "When I was a boy and I would see scary things in the news, my mother would say to me, 'Look for the helpers. You will always find people who are helping.'" The books in the display highlighted kindness, tolerance, and refugee and immigrant stories.

Brytani, from the Enoch Pratt Free Library in Baltimore, made a display for families to learn about Islam together. In addition to books, the librarian compiled a "fact file." This folder had articles from library databases that explain Islamic culture and customs, as well as a child-friendly explanation of the controversy over the word jihad. All the resources in the folder have their references listed, and there's a note indicating that families can take home copies of the articles and ask a librarian for more information.

Andria, from the Charleston County Public Library in South Carolina, created a display titled "Y'all Means All" for June for Pride month, but after the massacre at the gay nightclub in Orlando and the 2016 U.S. presidential election, she decided to make it a permanent display. In addition to the books, she has buttons and "wait a minute" flyers distributed throughout the library's Teen Lounge.

Front-Facing Fiascos

The American Library Association's Office for Intellectual Freedom began specifically tracking the censorship of library displays in December 2016. In some instances, a patron complained about the subject of a display, or about a specific book being included in display materials. Other complaints have been initiated internally from administrators, board members, or colleagues. When there are no policies to guide the librarians who have to respond to concerns about displays, often the display has been dismantled.

Temple, Texas

In June 2017, librarians at the Temple Public Library created a display to recognize June as GLBT Book Month. The library received few comments about the displays, but the issue gained steam after an Aug. 5 Facebook post by a local group, Concerned Christian Citizens, criticizing the display.

Fast-forward to the next library board meeting, where twenty-one residents spoke about the displays, beginning with former state representative Molly White. "Never, in my wildest dreams, did I ever imagine that my grandchildren would be exposed to materials that are not only contrary to personal growth, but leads people down a path of dysfunction and self-destruction," White declared. "Family units with a mother and father are the backbone of all society. Without strong, intact family units, societies will collapse."[3]

The month of June had been chosen to recognize LGBTQ pride to commemorate the Stonewall riots, which occurred at the end of June 1969. The Stonewall riots were multiple, violent demonstrations by members of the gay community in retaliation against a police raid that took place at the Stonewall Inn in Greenwich Village of New York City. Libraries and bookstores have been celebrating June as National Lesbian and Gay Book Month since the early 1990s. In 2015, the ALA's Office for Diversity, Literacy, and Outreach Services and the Gay, Lesbian, Bisexual, and Transgender Round Table (GLBTRT) continued the nationwide celebration with GLBT Book Month.

The controversy in Temple, Texas, was not the first time GLBT book displays have been targeted, and many times the displays have been taken down. The challengers' concern is less about the inclusion of diverse materials in the library collection than it is about the fact that librarians are choosing to display these materials, or promote them.

Anchorage, Alaska

In 2001, the Alaska Civil Liberties Union filed a lawsuit against the city of Anchorage after the mayor ordered the Z.J. Loussac Public Library's gay pride display removed for "advocating" a specific issue. Later, a court order required the reinstallation of the gay pride display for thirty days.[4]

> The First Amendment emphatically does not give mayors—or city council members, or legislators, or governors, or even presidents—the authority to restrain the presentation of exhibits at the library or any other public space. The First Amendment, and a huge body of law and tradition all over the United States, is intended to do the opposite—to

give all Americans the freedom to express themselves without fear that a misguided mayor may stop them.[5]

Hillsborough County, Florida

In 2006, another lawsuit[6] was filed after the Hillsborough County Commission voted to ban the county government from acknowledging gay pride. The members of the commission added this vote to their agenda after a Gay and Lesbian Pride Month display at the Tampa-Hillsborough County Public Library generated controversy. In 2013, the commissioners voted unanimously to repeal the ban of gay pride recognition in the county, including the public libraries.[7]

Rumford, Maine

Katrina Ray-Saulis, a resident of Rumford, shared an emotional discovery on Facebook when she learned that a Banned Books Week display at the Rumford Public Library was challenged by three local pastors.[8] In their letter to the library, the pastors were concerned about displaying "sexual themes that were not appropriate for children."[9] They asked the library administration "to have a high standard of providing and displaying books and resources that are high quality and promote high moral standards, especially where children are concerned." Others who supported the pastors were more open with their objections to the LGBTQ themes in the books that were displayed.

About a week after the library received the letter, the library board met to address the issue and provided opportunities for the public to present their opinions and concerns. With over seventy people in attendance, the trustees voted unanimously to keep the display intact.

This case received a great deal of national media and blog coverage because of the irony of wanting to ban a display that is specifically about banning books. In a post on the award-winning, nationally recognized LGBTQ parenting blog *Mombian*, Dana Rudolph concluded by saying: "Books matter. Representation matters. Community support matters. And librarians rock."[10]

The Right to Showcase

Displays are hard to classify because they are so broad in their definition and creators. Are displays considered art, and are they therefore expressive speech that merits First Amendment protection? If so, interior design, real

FIGURE 1.1 Rumford banned book display

estate staging, merchandising, and architecture might be considered art. The American Bar Association states that "visual art is as wide ranging in its depiction of ideas, concepts and emotions as any book, treatise, pamphlet or other writing, and is similarly entitled to full First Amendment protection."

Displays can also be considered as marketing or advertising. But since there's no profit involved, displays would not be considered commercial speech. Commercial speech is generally defined as speech designed to convince a target audience to purchase a good or service so that a business or individual can make a profit. The Supreme Court first explicitly ruled that truthful commercial speech was protected by the First Amendment in *Virginia Pharmacy v. Virginia Consumer Council.*[11]

Defending Displays

It is not uncommon for public library boards and academic institutions to adopt policies regarding the exhibits in their facilities. These policies have become more common since ALA crafted an interpretation of the *Library Bill of Rights* titled "Exhibit Spaces and Bulletin Boards."[12] (See "Exhibit Spaces and Bulletin Boards" and other interpretations of the *Library Bill of Rights* in the Appendix.)

Exhibit areas often are made available for use by community groups. Libraries should formulate a written policy for the use of these exhibit areas to assure that space is provided on an equitable basis to all groups that request it. Written policies for exhibit space use should be stated in inclusive rather than exclusive terms. For example, a policy that the library's exhibit space is open "to organizations engaged in educational, cultural, intellectual, or charitable activities" is an inclusive statement of the limited uses of the exhibit space. This defined limitation would permit religious groups to use the exhibit space because they engage in intellectual activities, but would exclude most commercial uses of the exhibit space.

Often these policies focus on the use of the exhibit space by external organizations. For example, the Forbes Library in Northampton, Massachusetts, has a policy that says: "The Forbes Library welcomes the opportunity to allow community groups and individuals to use the various display and exhibit areas in the building, as part of its mission to provide a wide range of information and materials, and to encourage and support the civic, intellectual, and cultural pursuits of the community."[13] Saint Louis University's exhibit policy says: "Although beliefs and viewpoints expressed in the displays belong to the exhibitors and do not necessarily represent the opinions of the Library Exhibits Committee or Saint Louis University Libraries, exhibits will be consistent with the University's educational philosophy and ideals and be fair and equitable concerning issues of potential controversy."[14] Neither of these policies outlines a procedure if there is a complaint about an item in the exhibit or about the topic of the display.

The Norfolk Public Library in Virginia has adopted a policy that not only references the ALA's "Freedom to Read" statement and the *Library Bill of Rights,* but also clearly states: "The library encourages free expression and free access to ideas, both essential elements in a democratic society, and does not knowingly discriminate regarding age, race, beliefs, or affiliations." The policy further states: "Exhibits will not be excluded because of the origin, background, or views of those contributing to their creation, nor removed because of partisan or doctrinal disapproval."[15] But the policy also includes a procedure in case an individual has a complaint about the exhibit: "The Norfolk Public Library's policy concerning challenged materials will be followed should complaints about an exhibit or display be received by the library.

The Norfolk Public Library Board of Trustees makes all final decisions re: challenged materials."

While the Norfolk Public Library's policy includes a strong endorsement of intellectual freedom, it doesn't specifically address the practice of displaying library materials around a topic that someone might find offensive. Librarians are more than a resource for finding materials of interest; they often advocate for the equality of underrepresented populations and for education on topics that are relevant to our culture and society.

Current Events Can Be Neutral

On February 14, 2018, a gunman entered a high school in Parkland, Florida, and killed seventeen people. The newspapers, talk shows, and social media were saturated with coverage of this tragedy. And in response to this school shooting, let's say that a librarian creates a display of library materials which includes the following works:

- *A Mother's Reckoning: Living in the Aftermath of Tragedy,* by Sue Klebold
- *An Unseen Angel: A Mother's Story of Faith, Hope and Healing after Sandy Hook,* by Alissa Parker
- *Be a Hero! The Essential Survival Guide to Active-Shooter Events,* by John Geddes
- *Books, Blackboards, and Bullets: School Shootings and Violence in America,* by Marcel Lebrun
- *Bowling for Columbine,* by Michael Moore
- *Citizen-Protectors: The Everyday Politics of Guns in an Age of Decline,* by Jennifer Carlson
- *Columbine,* by David Cullen
- *Enough: Our Fight to Keep America Safe from Gun Violence,* by Gabrielle Gifford
- *Give a Boy a Gun,* by Todd Strasser
- *Gun Control and the Second Amendment,* by Carol Hand
- *Gunman on Campus,* by Kim Etingoff
- *Gunned Down: The Power of the NRA,* by Michael Kirk
- *Nineteen Minutes,* by Jodi Picoult
- *School Shootings: What Every Parent and Educator Needs to Know to Protect Our Children,* by Joseph Lieberman

- *Surviving Columbine: How Faith Helps Us Find Peace When Tragedy Strikes,* by Liz Carlston
- *The Columbine Shootings,* by Diane Gimpel
- *The NRA Step-by-Step Guide to Gun Safety: How to Safely Care for, Use, and Store Your Firearms,* by Rick Sapp
- *The Spiral Notebook: The Aurora Theater Shooter and the Epidemic of Mass Violence Committed by American Youth,* by Stephen Singular

This hypothetical display is not a completely unbelievable possibility. It's even more plausible that someone, whether a patron who uses the library or an administrator or board member, would think that the display should be taken down. Having a policy and a proactive procedure in place for staff who create displays protects not only the library in case of a complaint, but also protects the staff member and her professional integrity.

Educating Exhibits Creators

It's easy to assume that all displays in libraries are going to be benign. But even the most benign or innocuous display may contain a book or other element that someone disapproves of. When complaints happen, administrators will need to defend the library's action in creating the display, and they may also need to defend the qualifications of the staff member who chose the items or the theme of the display. Moreover, administrators may need to state whether their permission was authorized to create something that represents the library. If a patron walks into the facility and takes a photograph of the display and posts it on social media, it will not be the staff member who created the display who will be blamed. It will be the institution as a whole and the director, dean, and board who are ultimately responsible.

The following are some questions to consider when outlining a procedure for creating displays:

- Are displays coordinated within individual buildings, or are they implemented at a system-wide level? At a school level? District level? Or at the university level?
- Is there a designated department that creates and manages the display? Or are staff in various departments responsible for contributing to the display?

- Is time provided for the staff to familiarize themselves with current displays?
- Is there a guideline for what tools to use or avoid, such as bookends, easels, materials, or props? Should the signage for a display follow a specific template or branding?
- Do all displays need to go through an approval process? Who has the authority to approve or disapprove them?
- Are there topics or materials (R-rated movies, profanity) that are off-limits in displays?
- If a topic is prohibited, who is responsible for deciding whether a display material falls within that category?
- Are your library's guidelines on displays available online? Are they available to all staff? Is the governing body aware of the guidelines?

Each library will have its own procedure for creating a display, and its own staff who are responsible for those displays. As a profession, we want to harness the talent and creativity of our skilled educators to create displays areas and physical spaces that are engaging and informative to our communities. Rather than stifle or undermine our colleagues' creativity and passion when complaints happen, we need to protect our libraries and staff by adopting values and principles that extend beyond the freedom to read, and reach into the freedom to teach, advocate, and engage.

Librarians are passionate and educated professionals who want to engage their communities and make a difference for the people they serve. But administrators are often pressured to keep any representation of the library neutral. To many, this neutrality does not mean that librarians have no values—we do.

When libraries vest the power of control in a policy or procedure to guide the operations of the library, the subjective power and privilege of one person is eliminated and the values of the library can shine through.

NOTES

1. Carol Smallwood, *Creative Management of Small Public Libraries in the 21st Century* (Lanham, MD: Rowman and Littlefield, 2014), 79.
2. Kelly Jensen, "Libraries Resist: A Round-Up of Tolerance, Social Justice, and Resistance in U.S. Libraries," Bookroit.com, February 10, 2017, https://bookriot.com/2017/02/10/libraries-resist-round-tolerance-social-justice-resistance-us-libraries.

3. Cody Weems, "Residents Divided over LGBT Library Display," *Temple Daily Telegram*, October 17, 2017, www.tdtnews.com/news/article_4d6f50dc-b388-11e7-983c-23c5941b656f.html.
4. "Gay-Pride Display Reinstalled at Anchorage Library," *American Libraries*, July 16, 2001, https://americanlibrariesmagazine.org/gay-pride-display-reinstalled-at-anchorage-library.
5. "June 9: The Anchorage Daily News chastises Mayor George Wuerch for banning a gay pride exhibit at the city's Loussac Library," *The Peninsula Clarion* (Kenai, AK), June 12, 2001.
6. Mary Minow, "Gay Display in Florida Library—Court Rules against First Amendment but Allows Discrimination (Equal Protection) Claim to Be Considered," *LibraryLaw* (blog), July 2006, http://blog.librarylaw.com/librarylaw/2006/07/gay_display_in_.html.
7. Norman Oder, "Florida County Bans 'Gay Pride,'" *Library Journal*, August 15, 2005; https://www.tampabay.com/news/localgovernment/public-hearing-under-way-over-hillsborough-county-ban-on-acknowledging-gay/2124940.
8. Katrina Ray-Saulis, "Mainers!" Facebook, September 14, 2018, https://www.facebook.com/KRaySaulis/posts/10217053091710089.
9. Bruce Farrin, "Rumford Public Library's Display of Banned Books Will Stay," *Sun Journal*, September 17, 2018, www.sunjournal.com/rumford-public-librarys-display-of-banned-books-will-stay.
10. Dana Rudolph, "Pastors Fail in Attempt to Remove LGBTQ Books from Banned Books Display," *Mombian* (blog), September 18, 2018, https://www.mombian.com/2018/09/18/pastors-fail-in-attempt-to-remove-lgbtq-books-from-banned-books-display/.
11. *Va. Pharmacy Bd. v. Va. Consumer Council*, 425 U.S. 748 (1976).
12. American Library Association, "Exhibit Spaces and Bulletin Boards," www.ala.org/advocacy/intfreedom/librarybill/interpretations/exhibit spaces.
13. Forbes Library, "Display/Exhibit Policy," https://forbeslibrary.org/info/policies/displayexhibit-policy.
14. Saint Louis University, "Library Exhibits Policy," http://lib.slu.edu/about/exhibit.
15. Norfolk Public Library, "Exhibit Policy," www.norfolkpubliclibrary.org/about-npl/policies/exhibit-policy.

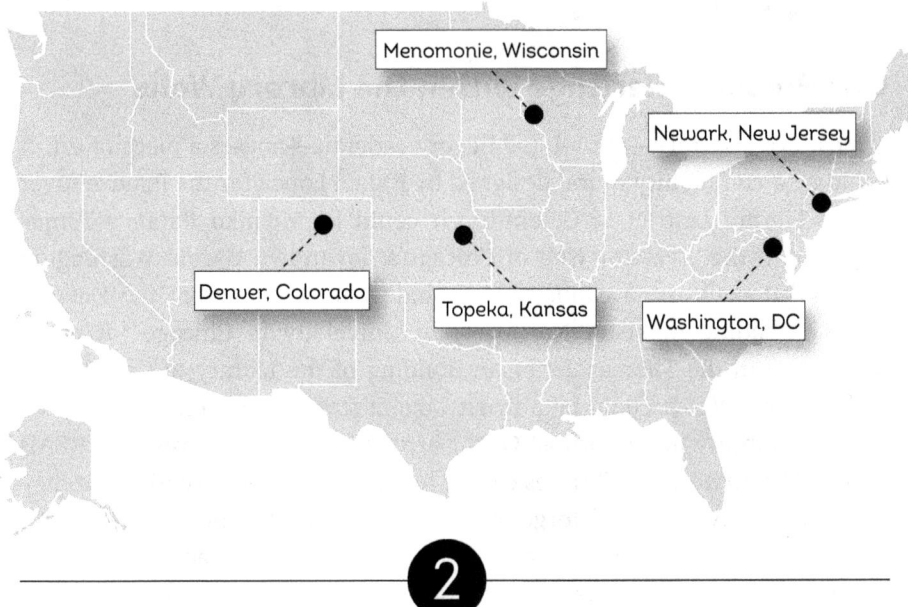

2

Artwork

"ART PREDATES THE WRITTEN WORD. IT REPRESENTS, DISPLAYS, and challenges cultural norms as well as bias and prejudice," said Jo Rolfe, director of the Camarillo Public Library and a former member of the ALA's Intellectual Freedom Committee. "Where better can we actively inspire abstract and concrete ideas, and the exploration of what it means to be human, than in the nation's libraries?"

Few would argue that the primary mission of libraries is to provide their communities with information. And information can be found in a wide variety of media, beyond just the books that have traditionally served as repositories of information. The artwork displayed in libraries is just a different way of presenting information.

Art is a nation's most precious heritage. For it is in our works of art that we reveal to ourselves and to others the inner vision which guides us as a nation. And where there is no vision, the people perish.

—Lyndon Johnson, on signing into existence
the National Endowment on the Arts

Our Precious Heritage within the Library Walls

Almost every library—school, public, or academic—houses a piece of art. It could be a community mural designed by Rafael Lopez for the Poudre River Public Library District in Colorado.[1] It could be Michiko Itatani's *Torque Sequence* in the escalator well of Chicago's downtown Harold Washington Library.[2] It could be a stained-glass window medallion from the Deering Library Reading Room at Northwestern University in Chicago.[3] It could be a quote in the Thomas Jefferson Building of the Library of Congress in Washington, DC.[4] It could be a Brian Goggin statue, *Speechless*, outside the Lafayette Library in California.[5] Or the artwork could just consist of a READ poster. The artworks in libraries can be highly visible and essential, but they can also be invisible and forgotten. A piece may have been chosen with deliberate care and in consultation with stakeholders, in accordance with library policy and after due consideration. Or a piece may have been inherited by generations of library staff who now never give it a second thought.

Beyond visual appeal, there are a number of reasons why artwork is installed in libraries. Illustrations and posters advocate for literacy and encourage frequent visits to the library to open a world of knowledge and information. Just as authors seek to have their stories read, artists and illustrators can showcase their ideas and their creativity by utilizing the passive audience that wanders the stacks. Artworks create a welcoming and engaging environment in the library.

Artwork hanging on the walls can be complemented by a conventional display. For example, if a library provides wall space for a local art photographer to showcase his or her work, the library could also create a book display on photography techniques, photography careers, well-known photographs, or the history of the photographs' subjects. Furthermore, libraries' arts programming frequently allows community members not only to view artworks, but to create them as well. Continuing with the photography example, perhaps the artist is invited to host a workshop on art photography. Community members thus become active, not passive, participants in the library's cultural programming.

Artwork often inspires collaborations between community partners like schools, health agencies, and civic and social organizations. The Pacific Beach Library hosts an innovative partnership between the library and the local art community in San Diego that leverages the library, with its lectures and exhibiting artists, as a community and cultural center.[6]

The galleries within libraries offer a space open to the community that stimulates visitors to experience the fine arts when they might not otherwise have prioritized it, thereby further enriching the library-going experience. Displaying community artwork or local artists' creations instills a sense of pride, not only in the art itself, but in being part of the community and the institution that produced and sponsored the art. And for youthful artists, the display of their creativity in a public space like a library, not out of obligation but of representation, will encourage their devotion to paint, draw, or make prints far more than any verbal praise could do. As respected institutions that are accessible to the entire spectrum of society, public, school, and academic libraries are in a unique position to highlight displays of art from all viewpoints, backgrounds, and perspectives.

Uncovering the Controversial

Throughout history, artwork has been altered, silenced, and censored due to its content, whether the motivations were religious, political, or because of the works' depictions of violence or nudity. At its core, art aims to make people think and feel, and these responses can be disturbing, confusing, and new. Given that works of art often evoke such diverse and passionate responses, it is not surprising that artistic expression has been the target of so many censorship efforts.

Sometimes, however, what is assumed to be a cause for concern turns out to be something entirely different. A high school librarian shared a story during a conference panel about the READ poster hanging in her media center which shows the musician and rapper Common holding Barack Obama's autobiography, *The Audacity of Hope*. A teacher complained to the principal about the poster and wanted it removed from the library walls. The librarian assumed that the concern

FIGURE 2.1
READ poster–Common

was based on some of Common's more controversial lyrics, but was surprised to discover that the problem was actually the book in the poster.[7] The teacher expressed concern that the school would be seen as biased and political if a poster was displayed with a book written by then-Senator Barack Obama. But because the teacher leaned to the political right, there was concern that her motivations were not fully objective or altruistic. Sometimes the reasons for censorship are clear and direct. But sometimes the reasons are entangled with ulterior motivations.

Menomonie, Wisconsin

There are three historical paintings by the Wisconsin artist Cal Peters which were commissioned under the Works Progress Administration in 1935. They have decorated the walls in Harvey Hall of the University of Wisconsin–Stout for over eighty years. The paintings depict French fur traders and American Indians traveling down the Red Cedar River by canoe.

In August 2016, the university's Diversity Leadership Team expressed concern that the paintings of the Indians would perpetuate racial stereotypes. The university chancellor, Bob Meyer, agreed with the team. Originally, he ordered the paintings to be removed and sent to the university's storage rooms in the basement, but later he announced that they would be relocated for display under "controlled circumstances." Because of the risk of "having a harmful effect on our students and other viewers," the paintings have been removed from Harvey Hall.

In a letter to Chancellor Meyer, the National Coalition Against Censorship wrote: "Such dialogue is especially important at a university, the quintessential 'marketplace of ideas.' A public university fails its educational mission when it eliminates material because some members of its community consider it offensive or objectionable. Such a paternalistic response from the university impinges on the academic freedom of the faculty and denies students important learning opportunities."[8]

Washington, DC

A painting by David Pulphus, a student at a Ferguson, Missouri, high school, hung in a hallway on Capitol Hill in Washington as one of more than 400 paintings that won an annual art competition. The painting portrays a police officer as a pig who is pointing a gun at black protesters—a representation meant to pay tribute to Michael Brown, who was killed by an officer in

Ferguson in 2014. Between January and April 2017, Republican lawmakers, with the support of House Speaker Paul Ryan, who called the painting "disgusting," repeatedly removed the painting, but the work was reinstated in the hallway each time by Missouri Representative Lacy Clay and other members of the Congressional Black Caucus. The Republican lawmakers' complaints finally prompted the architect of the Capitol, Stephen Ayers, to order the painting taken down.

In March of that year, Congressman Clay filed a lawsuit against the architect of the Capitol's decision to remove the student painting. A federal judge rejected Clay's request to rehang the controversial painting, saying, "There is little doubt that the removal of the painting was based on its viewpoint." But he concluded that the government's editorial decision to select and present the artwork meant that the display amounted to government speech and was, therefore, not subject to First Amendment protections."[9]

Denver, Colorado

As part of an educational outreach with the Denver Public Schools (DPS), the city of Denver displays art by students in the lobby of the Webb Building, a municipal building located downtown. In 2016, a picture depicting a police officer in a Ku Klux Klan hood pointing a gun at a black child whose hands are raised, while in the background, a hole torn in the U.S. flag reveals a Confederate flag, was chosen by a jury of community artists to be included in the DPS High School Art Exhibition along with other paintings, drawings, sculptures, and jewelry. The DPS doesn't have a policy restricting the art that students can create. Peter Castillo, the principal of the Kunsmiller Creative Arts Academy, said the school draws the line at vulgarity and profanity. "Outside of that," he said, "we embrace most of the creative process with artists."

The assignment for the 2016 exhibit was for students to research a work of art by one of the masters and then reinterpret it for modern times. The tenth-grade artist from Kunsmiller chose to reinterpret Francisco Goya's painting *The Third of May 1808,* which shows Napoleon's soldiers lined up in a firing squad and ready to execute a group of fearful Spanish civilians.[10] The artist said that she wanted her work to point to the Klan's history in Denver.

The student's work was also heavily influenced by Michael D'Antuono's 2014 painting *A Tale of Two Hoodies,* which shows a Klan-hooded police officer pointing a gun at a black child who is offering him a bag of candy.

After the tenth-grade artist learned that her painting was having a "negative impact," she requested that it be removed from the Webb Building exhibit.

The National Latino Police Officers Association called the picture "hate art," and the Denver Police Protective Association called it a "horrible stereotype." *The Denver Post* published an editorial from Svetlana Mintcheva, program director at the National Coalition Against Censorship, in which she states: "Police officers who risk their lives to protect the rest of us may be offended at such representations. But in our society, there is no right to not be offended, especially for those in public service, who should be open to critique by the community they serve."[11]

Newark, New Jersey

Kara Walker, a renowned African American artist who examines race, gender, sexuality, and violence, created a drawing entitled "The Moral Arc of History Ideally Bends towards Justice, but Just as Soon as Not Curves Back around toward Barbarism, Sadism, and Unrestrained Chaos." The drawing depicts the horrors of Reconstruction, twentieth-century Jim Crow, and the hooded figures of the Ku Klux Klan. In November 2012, the piece was loaned to the Newark Public Library by Scott London, a longtime art collector, and was displayed on the second floor.

The library has two galleries where an extensive collection is on view in several exhibitions a year. The library's holdings contain about 23,000 prints, including works by famous artists such as Picasso and Andy Warhol. Walker's drawing was initially covered after a library employee e-mailed the library director, Wilma Grey, that she had noticed a part of the drawing that shows a naked white man holding the head of a naked black woman to his groin. Several employees came to her expressing shock that the library would display such graphic artwork. Both the artist and the art collector were upset about the censorship.[12] "The library itself has a real history of engaging with art," Rachel Greene, of the New York consulting firm Art & Advisory, told *Art in America*. "But this is just so anti-art. Not everyone has to think [Walker] is a great artist, but the work should not be covered up."

In December 2012, Grey uncovered the censored artwork. Her intent was to turn it into a teaching moment by inviting the artist to visit the library, and promote education about Kara Walker and her work and about intellectual freedom.

Topeka, Kansas

The artist and teacher Tom Gregg exhibited fifteen still-life oil paintings called *Unsold: Grenades, Bad Apples, and Cute Animals* as part of a rotating artwork program at the University of Kansas Medical Center's Dykes Library. The most prominent object in each of these paintings is a hand grenade. Melissa Rountree, former curator of the Hallmark Art Collection, was informed by the interim head of the library that both the twenty-year-old exhibition program and her own position as curator were being discontinued. "On July 24, I got a call from an administrative assistant saying that the works needed to come down immediately."[13] Rountree was told that Gregg's artworks did not align with the core mission of the campus.

The ACLU of Kansas and Western Missouri, free speech and arts advocates, sent a letter to the University of Kansas's Board of Regents calling the decision to censor the exhibition program "constitutionally suspect" and a violation of "well-established principles of academic freedom." The Board of Regents and the University of Kansas chancellor's replies stated that the decision to not renew the contracts was a financial decision due to lack of state funding.

The First Amendment Right to Paint

The First Amendment of the U.S. Constitution prohibits government officials from suppressing speech based on the viewpoint it expresses. While initially interpreted to protect mainly political speech, interpretations gradually broadened to the point where today the First Amendment protects entertainment as well as the press, and images as well as words. Artistic expression, whether in films, paintings, or even video games, conveys views and opinions and thus participates in the democratic marketplace of ideas.

Although the First Amendment refers specifically to the freedoms of speech and the press, art forms—including paintings, illustrations, sculptures, tapestries, plays, music, dance, film, poetry, and graphic design—also enjoy considerable First Amendment protection. This doesn't mean that anything goes. The First Amendment's protections only apply to the government's restriction of the right to artistic expression and artistic reception. They do not protect against the restrictive actions of private citizens or businesses.

But libraries and schools, as public institutions, are obligated to protect the First Amendment right to expression and right to receive. The Supreme

Court and other courts have held conclusively that there is a First Amendment right to receive information; the right to receive information is a logical inference of the right to speak. Justice William Brennan elaborated on this point in 1965 regarding the case of *Lamont v. Postmaster General*:

> It is true that the First Amendment contains no specific guarantee of access to publications. However, the protection of the Bill of Rights goes beyond the specific guarantees to protect from congressional abridgment those equally fundamental personal rights necessary to make the express guarantees fully meaningful.
>
> I think the right to receive publications is such a fundamental right. The dissemination of ideas can accomplish nothing if otherwise willing addressees are not free to receive and consider them. It would be a barren marketplace of ideas that had only sellers and no buyers.[14]

The case of *Lamont v. Postmaster General* is a ruling on the delivery of mail by the U.S. Postal Service; and that government service, just like libraries, schools, city halls, government buildings, and public universities, is a public institution that is held to a higher obligation of freedom demanded by the First Amendment.

These public institutions and the government officials who work in them are called to a higher standard of public service and distance from personal opinions. Whether in the form of the library board, school administration, an elected representative, or a university dean, they must comply with the First Amendment's protection of art.

Not only does removing artwork from public spaces due to a complaint violate the First Amendment rights of the artist, it violates the right of the community that has the right to receive education and entertainment from visual forms of creative expression, which are protected as free speech. Legal cases have established precedents in exposing the liability that public institutions become vulnerable to when they remove protected works of art.

In 1997, the city of Murfreesboro, Tennessee, removed a painting of a nude from the Rotunda of City Hall after receiving a complaint that the display of the painting constituted sexual harassment.[15] The district court stated that the removal of the painting violated the artist's First Amendment rights:

The defendant's arbitrary decision to remove the painting of the plaintiff was guided by nothing other than the subjective perceptions of municipal officials. In this context, such an action banning protected expression based on a standardless discretion cannot be upheld as constitutional.

Our courts have time and again reaffirmed that the First Amendment prohibits public officials from censoring art that they find offensive or provocative. When libraries and public facilities open the door to displaying works of art, they are creating a "designated public forum." In such a forum, courts agree that the removal of artwork, based on its content, would only be justifiable under very limited circumstances.

"Content neutrality" comes into play when courts must decide a case involving freedom of expression. The government cannot limit expression just because any viewer, or even the majority of a community, is offended by its content. In the context of art and entertainment, this means tolerating many works that we might find offensive, insulting, outrageous—or just plain bad.

Exhibiting Excellence in Protecting Paintings

To provide professional guidance for librarian curators, the ALA adopted a *Library Bill of Rights* interpretation at the 2018 ALA Midwinter Meeting that emphasizes the role art plays in libraries, and emphasizes the need for libraries to present a broad spectrum of viewpoints in developing art exhibits and programs. The interpretation, "Visual and Performing Arts in Libraries," was written by the Intellectual Freedom Committee in consultation with artists, theater experts, and librarians and at the direction of Barbara Jones. (See "Visual and Performing Arts in Libraries" and other interpretations of the *Library Bill of Rights* in the Appendix.) Jones was the executive director of the ALA's Office for Intellectual Freedom from 2009 to 2015 and initiated this multiyear project before her retirement. The interpretation states:

> Libraries should not avoid developing exhibits or programs because of controversial content, or because of the beliefs or affiliations of those whose work is represented.
>
> Libraries that choose to make gallery or performing space available for use by community groups or individuals should formulate a written

22 | Chapter 2: Artwork

policy for the use of these areas and may adopt time, place, and manner rules for such use.

If users object to a particular work of art or performance there should be a method of recourse, similar to a reconsideration policy, for expressing their concerns.[16]

The National Coalition Against Censorship working directly with individual artists and curators involved in censorship disputes has created multiple resources to provide professional guidance where exhibits and artwork are in question. In the resource Artist Rights, a collaboration between the National Coalition Against Censorship and the Center for Democracy and Technology, the section on political speech states,

> Political speech is the core expressive activity that forms the foundation of our democracy; it receives the highest level of protection under the First Amendment. This protection includes art used in a political context, which covers everything from protest art to logos commissioned by political campaigns. It also protects art that contains political aspects but has no clear political message, such as art that lampoons a public figure for the way they dress (which might also be considered). In general, the First Amendment protects art with a political aspect unless it is found to be obscene or defamatory.[17]

Because so many controversies involve art that has an unpopular political viewpoint, when displaying any kind of art in a publicly funded institution, it is prudent to take steps that advance the library's mission, follow professional guidelines and adhere to the First Amendment.

Thoughtful Policies

The Hennepin County (MN) Library's community art display policy thoughtfully encourages and supports the inclusion of art in the library's buildings.

> Hennepin County Library recognizes that art has the power to enhance the quality of life of a community; it inspires citizens, contributes to civic pride and enlivens public places.
>
> The library is a unique and innovative venue for showcasing works

of art. Art enhances the patron relationship, contributes to a sense of place, and engages the mind. Community art exhibits encourage artists to engage in public life and moves people to see the world through a new and changing lens.[18]

While many libraries have adopted policies that list their selection criteria and the process for submitting public art proposals, very few policies address complaints or reference intellectual freedom or the *Library Bill of Rights*. The *Library Bill of Rights* is not just relevant for collection policies; it can be universally applied to all library resources, including the artwork that enhances libraries' physical spaces.

The Madison Public Library's (WI) art policy has a thorough and inclusive policy which states:

> Specific displays may include items that may be unorthodox or unpopular with the majority or controversial in nature. The Library's display of these items does not constitute endorsement of their content but rather makes available its expression. Madison Public Library adheres to the principles of intellectual freedom, adopted by the American Library Association, as expressed in the *Library Bill of Rights* and the Freedom to Read and Freedom to View Statements.[19]

The Madison Public Library's policy also addresses the process for review if a citizen expresses concern about a piece of art housed in the library's facilities. Outlining this process in a board-approved policy decreases the likelihood of censorship based on personal opinions and gut reactions. It also protects the library employees and board from having to personally approve each piece displayed. Artwork is incredibly subjective and difficult to judge under even the best of circumstances. But under public scrutiny and disapproval, the pressure to capitulate to complaints and challenges is intense. As outlined in the ALA *Code of Ethics* that guides professional standards, those charged with reviewing challenged resources, including artwork, should set aside their personal beliefs and evaluate the work in light of the objective standards outlined in the library's policy. (See the "ALA *Code of Ethics*" and other interpretations of the *Library Bill of Rights* in the Appendix.[20])

The following are some questions to consider when outlining how art is selected for a public institution:

- Are there specific sources that have a green light or red light by selectors?
- Are selections made by a committee/group or by a single person?
- How often are selections made or rotated?
- Are there different criteria for different age groups, locations, or formats?
- Are selections evaluated for copyright permissions?
- Are there images that are off-limits (violence, nudity)?
- Is approval required/recommended for all selections?
- What efforts are made to select diverse pieces?
- Are there public channels for submitting pieces or ideas for consideration?

Clear policies that outline how selections are made and that provide official recourse for users to express concerns are a necessary foundation, but often these policies are buried deep in a library's website or are unknown to the general public. Libraries should consider a small posting near exhibition areas that reiterates the library's vision and disclaims any endorsement of the works on display. Allowing our community members to express their opinions in a thoughtful, internal process dampens the potentially volatile eruption that becomes more likely if a citizen's only recourse is to post a picture on social media with an emotional rant and a demand for action.

Clear Procedure

Library administrators who consider implementing a visual arts program should approve a policy for dealing with art censorship issues and, as with traditional library materials, should brief staff members on how to handle complaints. Potentially controversial content shouldn't be automatically verboten; instead, it should be objectively dealt with on a piece-by-piece basis, long before an exhibit is installed. Each selection should be held to the same selection criteria that are used for all resources, with the aim of creating an enriching cultural and educational experience.

A common struggle with any challenge to library resources, specifically artwork, is when the complaint is initiated by a person who has political power. Having a clear procedure that applies to everyone, including even mayors and congressional representatives, can protect a library from folding under pressure.

Libraries should avoid words like "appropriate," "suitable nature," or "mature" in their selection and display policies. Every single person has a different understanding of what these words mean and what type of material they apply to. The guidelines and criteria listed in selection policies may restrict time, place, and manner use, but they should be content-neutral and equitable to all who request to use them.

The Eye of the Beholder

Art can be a beautiful thing, but it can also be ugly. At the Aurora Public Library in Illinois, a social media and press nightmare compelled the library board president to censor a satirical poem by a university philosophy professor. As part of a display of poetry and art, the professor's poem, "Hijab Means Jihad" was accused of hate speech and violence towards Muslims.[21] But his intent was rather different. His words, which were displayed against a Confederate flag, were meant to satirize the anti-Muslim perspectives that circulate harmfully through today's society. His work, protected by the First Amendment, was selected for display in the library and was installed for three weeks before complaints about it appeared on social media.

The library director, board president, and mayor considered their actions of censorship to be justified because their policy prohibited "material that threatens violence or intimidation of an individual or group." Librarians all over the country disagree about whether the poem qualifies as satire,

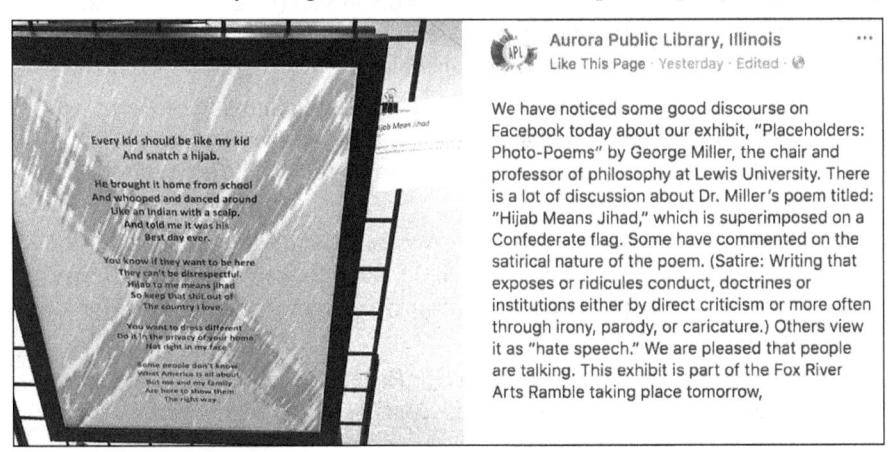

FIGURE 2.2 Aurora Poem

whether it should have been selected for display in the first place, and ultimately, whether the library administration's action in removing the piece was warranted.

NOTES

1. Urban Libraries Council, "Rafael Lopez Community Mural," https://www.urbanlibraries.org/innovations-old/2012-innovations/positioning-the-library/rafael-lopez-community-mural.
2. Chicago Public Library, "Art Tours of Harold Washington Library Center," https://www.chipublib.org/news/art-tours-of-harold-washington-library-center.
3. Northwestern University Library, "Reading Room Artwork," www.library.northwestern.edu/libraries-collections/deering-library/artwork/index.html.
4. Library of Congress, "On These Walls," https://www.loc.gov/loc/walls/jeff1.html.
5. Brian Goggin, "Speechless," www.metaphorm.org/portfolio/speechless.
6. Mark-Elliott Lugo, "Art for Libraries' Sake," *American Libraries* 30, no. 6 (June-July 1999).
7. Dan Zak, "Rapper Common Performs at White House amid Media Controversy," *Washington Post,* May 11, 2011, https://www.washingtonpost.com/lifestyle/style/rapper-common-performs-at-white-house-amid-media-controversy/2011/05/11/AFQHgcuG_story.html.
8. Jas Chana, "Uni. of Wisconsin-Stout Moves to Censor Paintings of First Nations People; UPDATE: Chancellor Modifies Course, Paintings to Be Relocated," *National Coalition Against Censorship* (blog), August 3, 2016, http://ncac.org/letters/university-of-wisconsin-stout-moves-to-censor-paintings-depicting-first-nations-people.
9. Sophie Tatum and Betsy Klein, "Controversial Painting to Be Removed from Capitol," CNN, January 14, 2017, https://www.cnn.com/2017/01/13/politics/controversial-painting-to-be-removed-from-capitol/index.html.
10. Noelle Phillips, "Denver Student's Artwork Removed from Show for KKK Cop Portrayal," *Denver Post,* March 23, 2016, https://www.denverpost.com/2016/03/23/denver-students-artwork-removed-from-show-for-kkk-cop-portrayal.
11. Svetlana Mintcheva, "Does 'Hate Art' Have a Place?" *Denver Post,* March 24, 2016, https://www.denverpost.com/2016/03/24/does-hate-art-have-a-place.
12. Brian Boucher, "Kara Walker Artwork Censored at Newark Library,"

Art in America, December 11, 2012, https://www.artinamericamagazine.com/news-features/news/kara-walker-newark-library; Barry Carter, "Censorship or Common Decency? Newark Library Covers Up Controversial Artwork," *NJ.com* (blog), December 2, 2012, http://blog.nj.com/njv_barry_carter/2012/12/censorship_or_common_decency_n.html.

13. Svetlana Mintcheva, "Kansas Board of Regents Must Overturn Exhibit Takedown," *National Coalition Against Censorship* (blog), August 8, 2013, http://ncac.org/incident/arts-avocacy-project-kansas-board-of-regents-must-overturn-exhibit-takedown; Laura Spencer, "Exhibition Program Halted at KU Medical Center," KCUR, August 28, 2013, http://kcur.org/post/exhibition-program-halted-ku-medical-center#stream/0.
14. *Lamont v. Postmaster General*, 381 U.S. 301 (1965).
15. Henderson v. City of Murfreesboro, 960 F. Supp. 1292 (1997); Leagle, "Henderson v. City of Murfreesboro, Tenn," https://www.leagle.com/decision/19972252960fsupp129212088.
16. American Library Association, "Visual and Performing Arts in Libraries," www.ala.org/advocacy/intfreedom/librarybill/interpretations/arts.
17. National Coalition Against Censorship and the Center for Democracy and Technology, "Artists Rights," www.artistrights.info/political-speech.
18. Hennepin County Library, "Community Art Display Policy," https://www.hclib.org/about/policies/community-art-display-policy.
19. Madison Public Library, "Art Policy," https://www.madisonpubliclibrary.org/policies/art-policy.
20. American Library Association, "Professional Ethics," www.ala.org/tools/ethics.
21. "Art Criticized as Anti-Muslim Removed from Aurora Public Library," ABC7, April 22, 2018, http://abc7chicago.com/society/art-criticized-as-anti-muslim-removed-from-aurora-public-library/3379404.

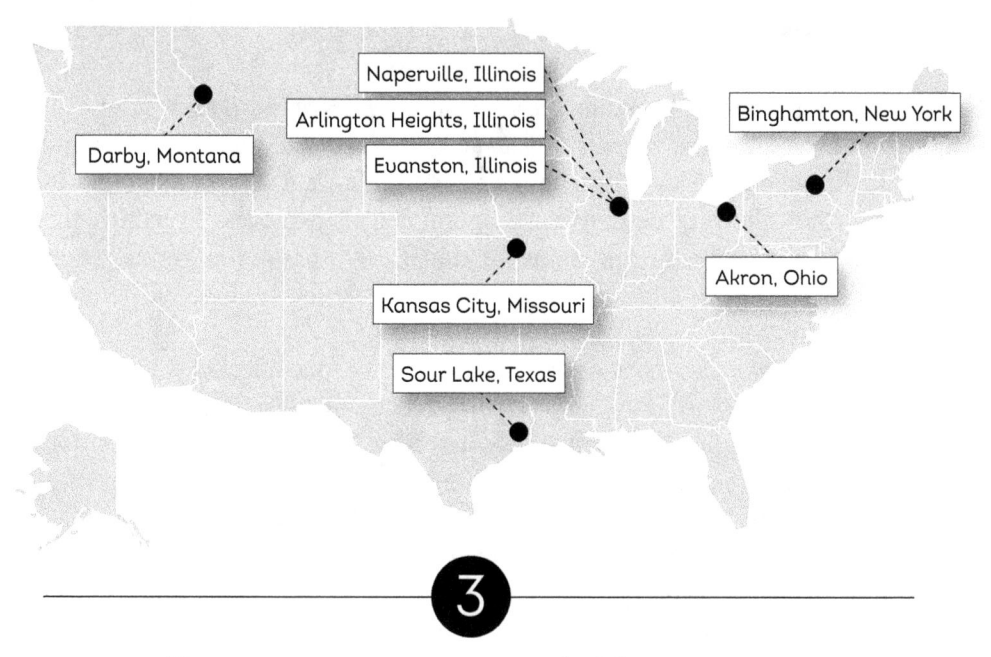

Map locations: Darby, Montana; Naperville, Illinois; Arlington Heights, Illinois; Evanston, Illinois; Binghamton, New York; Akron, Ohio; Kansas City, Missouri; Sour Lake, Texas

3

Programs and Events

IN A PIECE TITLED "PARADISE IS PAPER, VELLUM, AND DUST," THE author and columnist Ben Macintyre wrote that "libraries are not just for reading in, but for sociable thinking, exploring, exchanging ideas, and falling in love. They were never silent. Technology will not change that, for even in the starchiest heyday of Victorian self-improvement, libraries were intended to be meeting places of the mind, recreational as well as educational."[1] Macintyre's enchanting prose breathes new life into the vision of the old stereotype of the library. Where some might see stale air, he sees the swirl of romance and possibilities.

Essential Service for Everyone

Libraries have offered programs to their communities long before there was Facebook to share events; the internet to post details about them; the microphone to project speakers' voices; the telephone to schedule performances; and cars to transport supplies. It was about the mid-1960s when our profession started educating about and discussing programs as a service to the community, just like reference interviews, reading instruction, research, and readers' advisory.

In Brett Lear's book *Adult Programs in the Library*, he does a masterful job of combining the *Webster's Dictionary* multipart definition of "program" with the Public Library Association's 1979 definition of "information" to create the following definition: "Programming is a process by which the informational, educational, and recreational needs of your patrons are met by bringing patrons into contact with the human resources best able to meet those needs."[2]

Nevertheless, for most of the general public, the idea of visiting the library for an event, program, or performance—whether cultural, educational, or recreational—is a relatively new idea. The long-standing tradition of children's storytimes has monopolized the public's understanding of a program. Now, libraries' programming[3] has exploded in all directions. The age of the target audience has expanded greatly: from baby lap time, tween coding workshops, young adult anime clubs, twenty-something trivia nights, adult bike repair co-ops, and baby boomer investment tutorials, to seniors who do yoga. Programs have also expanded in terms of their space considerations, destination, materials, content, skill level, audience, and performers. No idea is out of bounds anymore.

Programming is initiated by all types of libraries and other public institutions:[4] public libraries, schools, universities, museums, parks, and local governments. Therefore, any institution or organization that is publicly funded is held to the highest standard of freedom guaranteed to people by the First Amendment.

The creativity and passion that radiate from programming librarians are contagious and inspiring. They are reaching beyond the four walls of the building and the stereotypes of library materials and services, and are trying to engage the community and transform its members' information and social needs. And inevitably, sometimes librarians push the envelope beyond what some in the community may be ready for.

Controversy on the Calendar

Reports of censorship of programming have increased exponentially. Historically, we would see complaints about Harry Potter parties, and canceled book clubs because of books with LGBTQ or fantasy content. But the trends have now shifted to disinviting authors and censoring programs that offer educational content about sexual topics. And most notably, with LGBTQ being the number-one reason for censorship in libraries, reports are pouring in about drag queen storytimes and gay authors.

Darby, Montana

Wendy Campbell, director of the Darby Public Library, shared her experience with the attempted censorship of a library program, in an article in *American Libraries*. In 2016, the library hosted a series of cultural lectures, including one on "Perspectives on Islam" by an Arabic languages professor that was preceded by angry complaints and hostile accusations. Some members of the small community of 4,000 visited the library to submit written complaint forms, and they took forms with them to get other like-minded neighbors to express their opposition to the lecture. One community member commented that "all Muslims sought to kill us, and that we were at war with Islam."[5]

The Darby school and library boards held meetings so that community members could share their concerns about the program. Ultimately, the programs at the high school and the public library continued and were incredibly successful. When Campbell introduced Professor Samir Bitar to the meeting room, which was filled to maximum capacity, she said:

> We live in the Land of the Free where we enjoy freedom of speech and the freedom to be educated in our topics of interest. And we are the Home of the Brave, where we are not afraid of different viewpoints or ideas. We welcome them so that we may be educated and make informed decisions. And we live in the West, in Montana, in Darby, where we are open and polite and welcoming to others. With that, I ask you to help me welcome our speaker tonight.

Later in 2016, Campbell received the University of Illinois at Urbana-Champaign's Downs Intellectual Freedom Award for her unwavering resolve to turn the controversial event into an opportunity for respectful dialogue.

Sour Lake, Texas

The filmmaker and author e.E. Charlton-Trujillo was disinvited from speaking at a middle school in a small town in Texas. Her third novel, *Fat Angie* (2013), is an emotional and humorous story about an overweight teenager who attempts suicide and later falls in love with the new girl in town. Charlton-Trujillo's documentary film, *At-Risk Summer*, records her experience of embarking on a self-funded, unconventional book tour across America to hold writing workshops with at-risk youth.

Charlton-Trujillo had been corresponding with the librarian of the middle school for months after being invited to speak to the students about *Fat Angie*, which won the Stonewall Award given by the ALA's Gay, Lesbian, Bisexual, and Transgender Round Table, and about her documentary film, which also features award-winning authors Laurie Halse Anderson, Meg Medina, Kathy Erskine, A. S. King, Matt de la Peña, Ellen Hopkins, and Michele Embree.

Four days before the event, Charlton-Trujillo was e-mailed to cancel the visit. All of her books that had been preordered for the students in anticipation of her visit were returned to the bookstore.[6] Silence from the middle school and school district left Charlton-Trujillo concerned and confused. Finally, the principal replied with "scheduling conflict" as an excuse for censoring this school library program.

Binghamton, New York

In January 2018, the Broome County Public Library publicized a Drag Queen Story Time for all ages that would have drag princess characters visiting the library and reading to kids.[7] Public comments—mostly opposing, but some supporting—quickly started arriving. Some comments were posted on Facebook, some were sent via e-mail, and some were delivered in person, and the library director, Lisa Wise, received so many phone calls with sentiments of "you're going to hell" that she stopped answering and let her voicemail pick up. One Facebook commenter stated: "This is SICK. It is the parents' duty

---

Broome County Public Library
January 8

Throughout their history, American public libraries have been on the front lines of the fight to dispel ignorance, intolerance, and bigotry.

We are following in the footsteps of the greatest of public libraries, the New York Public Library, in holding an event of this nature and we are pleased to have received the positive feedback we have from families excited to attend the story time.

Our library continues to broaden horizons and to celebrate the diversity of our culturally rich community here in the Southern Tier. We are committed to providing programming that appeals to diverse elements of our community.

Libraries stand for values of freedom, intellect, openness, tolerance, and the opportunity to freely explore the entirety of the world in which we live. If any of our enrichment programs offend the sensibilities of some of our patrons, they are welcome to exercise their freedom to not participate.

192   25 Comments 18 Shares

**FIGURE 3.1
Screenshot of Broome County Facebook post**

to protect their children from such depravity. I can't believe our county is promoting such filth." Another user said, "Sickening. You people are monsters." A self-identified nonprofit Christian charity, the New Yorker's Family Research Foundation, released a statement against the event that "calls upon the Broome County Public Library to cancel this event, and we also respectfully encourage parents not to expose their children to it."[8]

In response, the library administration proudly defended the program on Facebook.[9] With the full support of the library board, the library welcomed over 200 children and families along with Elsa, Ariel, Merida, Wonder Woman, and Jasmine to bring their favorite characters to life, look beyond gender stereotypes, and exemplify inclusion.

Kansas City, Missouri

In an event titled "Truman and Israel," co-presented by the Kansas City Public Library, the Truman Library Institute, and the Jewish Community Foundation of Greater Kansas City, Ambassador Dennis Ross, a U.S. diplomat to the Middle East who had served in the Obama, Clinton, and George H. W. Bush administrations, spoke about American policy and Israeli security and the presidential history of their relationship.

During the Q&A session following the lecture, a social activist attending the program asked a question that led to a series of excessive repercussions. Cell phone and security video footage shows the off-duty police (who were acting as private security hired by one of the sponsors of the lecture series) arresting both the activist and the library's director of public programming, Steve Woolfolk.[10] Woolfolk had intervened when security initially tried to remove the patron; he was simply trying to deescalate the situation and explain the library's procedure for public events. Later, Woolfolk was informed that his official charge was "interfering with a police action." It is unclear why security reacted so strongly and why they felt entitled to assert wrongful control over a participant's questions at a public event.

In a brief trial four months after the event, a municipal court judge found Woolfolk not guilty on charges of obstruction, interfering with an arrest, and assaulting a police officer. The Kansas City Public Library's director, Crosby Kemper III, publicly stated, "The library, like the judge, has consistently expressed surprise that this ever went to trial, that a public event at a public library should result in the indictment of a librarian."[11]

Naperville, Illinois

In 2009, the Naperville North history teacher Kermit Eby invited his former University of Illinois – Chicago education professor, Bill Ayers, to speak with his high school students. Ayers, a radical social activist and author, had been a founding member of the violent anti-Vietnam War group known as the Weather Underground in the late 1960s. He now teaches educational reform, curriculum, and instruction.

The invitation to Ayers provoked a public outcry. Critics commenting on newspaper websites and contacting school administrators repeatedly referred to Ayers as a "terrorist," and the school received hundreds of angry e-mails and voicemails. Despite requiring students to produce parental permission slips to hear Ayers speak, the school felt that his past actions outweighed any benefit to future discussion, and so the superintendent canceled Ayers's appearance. In addition to the event at Naperville North High School, Ayers had been scheduled to appear at Boston College and Anderson Bookstore; but because of the outcry, these events were also canceled. Ayers was quoted in Chicago's *Daily Herald* newspaper as saying, "It has all the hallmarks of suppression of speech: incitement of fear, intimidation of well-meaning folks, mob rule."[12]

Arlington Heights, Illinois

The Arlington Heights Memorial Library organized a presentation from the Community Activism Law Alliance entitled "Know Your Rights," which was focused on informing undocumented residents, and anyone else, about their legal rights with law enforcement.[13] At the presentation, legal counsel would update the attendees about what recent presidential executive orders meant for immigrants, and would discuss the preparations for those at risk of being detained or deported. Days before the presentation, the program was canceled on account of "safety issues." In actuality, residents had threatened to sue the library and report the program to U.S. Immigration and Customs Enforcement (ICE). Their communications included demands for the firing of the library director and promises to hold protests with like-minded residents. But in fact, the protest turned out to be in favor of the library's program and immigrants. The Saturday after the canceled program, more than 100 people rallied outside the Arlington Heights Memorial Library in peaceful support of immigration and the library, and in denunciation of hate and racism.[14]

Evanston, Illinois

The Evanston Public Library invited the Palestinian-American author Ali Abunimah to read from his book *The Battle for Justice in Palestine* and discuss international events. But the library director canceled the speaking engagement.[15] After accusations of censorship and political bias by the author and the public, the library reinvited the author.

More than 120 people packed into the conference room, with a police presence inside and outside the library. But the tone was peaceful as Abunimah described the Gaza Strip and its economy and travel conditions. Over 100 people were at an overflow location, which was added after the event filled to capacity, and even more were turned away from the library before the program because the conference room's maximum capacity had been reached.[16]

Akron, Ohio

The Akron-Summit County Public Library invited the author Matt Taibbi to speak in November 2017.[17] The program was to discuss Taibbi's new book, *I Can't Breathe*, about 43-year-old Eric Garner, a black man who died in 2014 after being placed in a chokehold by members of the New York City Police Department.

A week before the scheduled event, the library canceled the event because of something that Taibbi had written seventeen years earlier in a book titled *The Exile: Sex, Drugs and Libel in the New Russia*. The library notified its newsletter subscribers and posted the cancellation on Facebook, writing: "Over the past week, Mr. Taibbi's writings about his time in Russia have come under scrutiny, particularly a book he coauthored in 2000 that contains graphic misogynistic imagery involving the sexual exploitation of women."[18]

Taibbi had issued an apology earlier that month for his past behavior, and later many of the sources of the accusations were exposed. An article in *Paste Magazine* stated: "Matt Taibbi has never been accused by any woman of sexual assault or impropriety. The women he is accused of harassing (those who weren't fictional) based on satirical passages from a book he coauthored nearly two decades ago, have all denounced the allegations."[19]

The Right to Speak and the Right to Program

Free speech rights are often predicated on the environment where the individual or organization is speaking. Much of the confusion over the extent of these rights, and an individual's expectations, can be dispelled by determining if the environment is a "public forum" and what type of public forum it is. There are three types of public forums:

1. A "traditional," or "open, public forum" is a place with a long tradition of freedom of expression, such as a public park or a street corner. The government can normally impose only content-neutral time, place, and manner restrictions on speech in a public forum. Restrictions on speech in a public forum that are based on content will be struck down, unless the government can show that the restriction is necessary to further a compelling governmental interest.
2. A "limited public forum" or "designated public forum" is a place with a more limited history of expressive activity, usually only for certain groups or topics. Examples of a limited public forum would include a university meeting hall, a city-owned theater, or a library. The government can limit access to certain types of speakers in a limited public forum, or limit the use of such facilities for certain subjects. Despite these more proscriptive guidelines, however, a governmental institution may still not restrict expression at a limited forum unless that restriction serves a "compelling interest."
3. A "closed public forum" is a place that, traditionally, has not been open to public expression, such as a jail or a military base. Governmental restrictions on access to a nonpublic forum will be upheld as long as they are reasonable and not based on a desire to suppress a particular viewpoint. This standard is far more deferential to government officials.

The events and programs hosted by a public library, school, public museum, or university are usually considered a "limited public forum" in that they have been solicited by the library to meet the educational and entertainment needs outlined by the library's mission and, hopefully, its programming policy. Many factors are considered when creating public programming: the availability of knowledgeable speakers or talented performers, the public's desire/demand for the content, the targeted audience, financial resources, space restrictions, and supplies and staff time. The ultimate goal is to provide access to new ideas, different learning methods, and open discussion for the community.

There is no specific case law that outlines the right to attend a public program or that outlines the right of a library to host a public program. There was a case in 1972, *Kleindienst v. Mandel*, that addressed the question of whether the public had a right to hear a speaker's ideas in person.[20] Attorney General Richard Kleindienst denied a visa to Ernest Mandel, a Belgian journalist and Marxist theoretician, who had been invited to participate in academic conferences and discussions in the United States. As to whether the international speaker's rights had been violated, the Supreme Court strongly implied a constitutional interest on the part of potential citizen audiences but ultimately held that in this case Mandel wasn't granted US First Amendment protections. When the claim was made that people could buy his books and read his speeches, Justice Harry Blackmun argued that "this argument overlooks what may be particular qualities inherent in sustained, face-to-face debate, discussion and questioning." Justice Thurgood Marshall agreed, stating that "the right to speak and hear—including the right to inform others and to be informed about public issues—are inextricably part of that process."[21]

Earlier cases involving academic speaker cancellations and bans did imply a right to hear. In most cases of the late 1960s and early 1970s, the speaker was among the plaintiffs, so the rights of the audience never came into issue.[22] In one case, however, the speaker had dropped out of the suit. The court nonetheless went on to strike down the speaker ban at the request of the prospective listeners. In their *Snyder v. Board of Trustees of University of Illinois* opinion, the judges wrote:

> There is respectable authority indicating that the audience, which is, after all, a principal beneficiary of the First Amendment, also has standing to seek relief against illegal censorship. . . . There is a First Amendment right to peacefully assemble to listen to the speaker of one's choice, which may not be impaired by state legislation any more than the right of the speaker may be impaired.[23]

In a 1985 Supreme Court case about live entertainment, the justices' opinion stated that "entertainment, as well as political and ideological speech, is protected; motion pictures, programs broadcast by radio and television, and live entertainment, such us musical and dramatic works, fall with the First Amendment guarantee."[24] After all, "one man's amusement, teaches another's doctrine."

If a citizen of the United States is guaranteed the right to read and access information from the public library, doesn't the librarian have a constitutional right, even a responsibility, to serve that interest? Programs are a significant source of information. Some programs are providing access to information and perspectives that are marginalized or silenced. The demand for guidance in how to defend programs is rising. Traditionally librarians bear considerable pressure to adhere to the norm and not push the envelope. As that begins to change and more "radical librarians" push the status quo with drag queen storytimes, political speakers, and social justice advocates, the need for guidance and safeguards against censorship will also rise.

Supporting Programming Librarians

To provide superior programming in public institutions, protecting and defending the creative skills of event planners must be a priority. Just as librarians consider a selection policy when purchasing books, DVDs, databases, and journals that will circulate well, be informative and authoritative, meet the educational needs of a wide variety of audiences, and provide diverse viewpoints, librarians must also utilize these same professional skills in organizing programs.

It's not uncommon for programming librarians to hold a significant level of autonomy, or freedom, in their ideas for bringing people to the library and presenting them with new information and different points of view. In an informal survey in a Facebook group for programming librarians,[25] the most consistent response was the importance of communication between staff and administrators during the developmental process for all programs. Building that trust is essential to maintaining a level of autonomy for the programming librarian. And while librarians may hold that autonomy by practice and procedure, a recommended best practice is for libraries and other public institutions to have a policy that clearly defines that autonomy, outlines who is ultimately responsible, what the criteria are for selection and rejection, and how people can express comments.

Because of the paucity of institutional safeguards to protect the freedom of librarians to explore seemingly controversial topics, speakers, and books, many librarians don't stray too far outside the acceptable box. And there is, in fact, very little support for the constitutional claim that librarians have the "right" to provide knowledge through programming.

The ALA's *Library Bill of Rights* has been updated with a 2018 interpretation which emphasizes the role that programs play in supporting the mission of the library, by providing users with additional opportunities for accessing information, education, and recreation.[26] The interpretation, "Library-Initiated Programs as a Resource," states: "Libraries should not avoid developing exhibits or programs because of controversial content, or because of the beliefs or affiliations of those whose work is represented." (See "Library-Initiated Programs as a Resource" and other interpretations of the *Library Bill of Rights* in the Appendix.)

The Public Library of Cincinnati and Hamilton County (OH) has adopted a thorough policy that is exemplary in its support of library staff, and which clearly outlines who has the responsibility and authority for program implementation.[27] In addition to stating the purpose of library programs, the policy also expounds on the process of choosing programs and the expansive range of possibilities that is not limited by possible controversy: "Library sponsorship of a program does not constitute an endorsement of the content of the program or the views expressed by participants, and program topics, speakers and resources are not excluded from programs because of possible controversy."

The Gail Borden Public Library District in Illinois has broadened its selection policy beyond materials to include all resources, including "public programs, exhibits, displays and public announcement postings."[28] Instead of adopting and maintaining multiple policies, the district has adopted the principles of intellectual freedom while using almost identical procedures for how the staff select materials, resources, and services and how they address concerns.

Just like all resources and materials in libraries, programs can elicit concerns and opinions from the public. Policies that encourage feedback and provide an outlet for the community to express its concerns are the first and most important step in managing communication. Having a procedure in place for routing and addressing concerns reassures community members that they are being heard and that their opinions and concerns are valued.

Whether a library chooses a unique procedure or relies on the existing reconsideration policies, these systems can manage a significant majority of concerns that may arise.

The following are some questions to consider when writing a programming policy:

- Are there limitations to program formats or locations (outside, off-site, or nonpublic areas)?
- Can programs be limited to specific age groups?
- If libraries require registration for programs, are these records anonymized or destroyed afterward in order to protect patrons' privacy?
- Is there a process for considering non-library-initiated programs from groups or individuals?
- What funding sources are acceptable to sponsor programs (commercial or political organizations)?
- Has the library reflected on systemic bias when evaluating programs?
- How are conflicts of interest disclosed?
- Are programs being considered that welcome underrepresented populations?

Policies and procedures don't just help protect the library. Strong programming policies that embrace intellectual freedom and don't shy away from controversy also protect the programming staff. Knowing that the library administration has a backbone of strength and support can increase the staff's confidence and trust. For many professionals who lack a declaration of support or a process for managing complaints, there is an underlying fear that any controversy could result in canceling a program, disciplinary action, or even possible termination.

Bias vs. Balance

The debate over neutrality in libraries and educational institutions has been going on for a long time and will continue to do so. But there is a subtle shift in how libraries are defining their position in their policies. Older library policies would often state that any topic touching on politics or religion, or anything controversial, wouldn't be permissible if the public library were to maintain neutrality. The more current policies that guide programming staff are trending towards a more narrow definition of what is prohibited. The Midlothian Public Library (IL) programming policy states: "The library does not offer any programs that support or oppose any political candidate, ballot measure, or specific religious conviction. Programs whose purpose is to provide information about religious traditions as a part of multicultural education are permitted."[29] The Wells Public Library (ME) programming policy states: "The library does not offer programs that support or oppose any political candidate or ballot measure. However, election information, such as candidates' forums that include invitations to all recognized candidates, may be offered."[30]

Libraries should be free to offer programming on a wide variety of topics that educate communities and encourage conversation and the sharing of ideas. By limiting topics to only what is safe and noncontroversial, successful library programs like "Librarians vs. Fake News,"[31] "Voterpalooza," and "Civic Saturdays"[32] would be lost to the world because they are political.

NOTES

1. Ben Macintyre, "Paradise Is Paper, Vellum, and Dust," *Times Online,* December 18, 2004.
2. Brett W. Lear, *Adult Programs in the Library* (Chicago: American Library Association, 2013).
3. National Impact of Library Public Programs Assessment, "An Exploration of U.S. Library Public Programs," https://NILPPA.org.
4. The Law Dictionary, "Public Institution," https://thelawdictionary.org/public-institution.
5. Wendy Campbell, "Perspectives on Islam in Montana," *American Libraries,* April 15, 2016, https://americanlibrariesmagazine.org/2016/04/15/perspectives-islam-montana.
6. Curious City, "Uninvited," https://www.curiouscity.net/uninvited.
7. "Drag Queen-Themed Event at Broome County Public Library Sparks Controversy," WBNG.com, date, www.wbng.com/story/37219933/drag-queen-themed-event-at-broome-county-public-library-sparks-controversy.
8. New Yorker's Family Research Foundation, "Binghamton Library Should Be for Books, Not Drag Shows," https://www.newyorkfamilies.org/public-libraries-books-not-drag-shows/.
9. Broome County Public Library, "Drag Queen Story Time," Facebook, January 8, 2018, https://www.facebook.com/events/1172212276245737/permalink/1173801519420146.

10. George M. Eberhart, "Kansas City Public Library Embroiled in Free-Speech Case," *American Libraries*, October 3, 2016, https://americanlibraries magazine.org/blogs/the-scoop/kansas-city-public-library-embroiled-in -free-speech-case/.

11. Lisa Peet, "Kansas City Libraries Defend Free Speech in Face of Arrests, Resignations," *Library Journal*, September 9, 2017, https://lj.libraryjournal .com/2017/09/industry-news/kansas-city-libraries-defend-free-speech-in -face-of-arrests-resignations.

12. Office for Intellectual Freedom, "Naperville Illinois," *Newsletter on Intellectual Freedom*, May 2009, 3.

13. Christopher Placek, "Decision to Cancel Immigration Rights Event Upsets Arlington Heights Residents," *Daily Herald*, October 4, 2017, https:// www.dailyherald.com/news/20171003/decision-to-cancel-immigration -rights-event-upsets-arlington-heights-residents.

14. Karen Ann Cullotta, "Pro-Immigration Rally Held at Arlington Heights Library That Received Threatening Phone Calls," *Chicago Tribune*, September 30, 2017, www.chicagotribune.com/suburbs/arlington-heights/news/ ct-ahp-arlington-library-immigration-rally-tl-1005–20170930-story.html.

15. Alice Yin, "Evanston Public Library Reinstates Canceled Book Talk after Accusations of Censorship," *Daily Northwestern*, August 4, 2014, https:// dailynorthwestern.com/2014/08/04/city/evanston-public-library-reinstates -canceled-book-talk-after-accusations-of-censorship/.

16. Lisa Black, "Pro-Palestinian Chicago Writer Addresses Peaceful Crowd at Evanston Library," *Chicago Tribune*, August 11, 2014, www.chicagotribune .com/suburbs/evanston/chi-pro-palestinian-writer-evanston-library-2014 0811-story.html.

17. Jennifer Conn, "Akron-Summit County Library Cancels Matt Taibbi Appearance over Past Misogynistic Writings," Cleveland.com, November 8, 2017, https://www.cleveland.com/akron/index.ssf/2017/11/ akron-summit_county_library_ca.html.

18. Akron-Summit County Public Library, "The Main Event Program Scheduled for Thursday, November 9 at Main Library, Featuring Author Matt Taibbi, Has Been Cancelled," Facebook, November 7, 2017, www.facebook .com/AkronLibrary/posts/10156860027906038.

19. Walker Bragman, "The Destruction of Matt Taibbi," *Paste Magazine*, December 11, 2017, https://www.pastemagazine.com/articles/2017/12/ the-destruction-of-matt-taibbi.html.

20. *Kleindienst v. Mandel*, 408 U.S. 753 (1972).

21. Robert M. O'Neil, "Libraries, Librarians, and First Amendment Freedoms," *Articles by Maurer Faculty* (1975).

22. William W. Van Alstyne, "Political Speakers at State Universities: Some Constitutional Considerations," *University of Pennsylvania Law Review* 328–42 (1963), https://scholarship.law.duke.edu/faculty_scholarship/565.
23. *Snyder v. Board of Trustees of University of Illinois*, 286 F. Supp. 927 (N.D. Ill. 1968).
24. *Schad v. Borough of Mount Ephraim* 452 US 61, 65 (1985).
25. Programming Librarian Interest Group, Facebook, https://www.facebook.com/groups/ProgrammingLibrarianInterestGroup/.
26. American Library Association, "Library-Initiated Programs as a Resource," www.ala.org/advocacy/intfreedom/librarybill/interpretations/programs.
27. Public Library of Cincinnati and Hamilton County, "Policies—Library Programs," https://www.cincinnatilibrary.org/policies/programs.html.
28. Gail Borden Public Library District, "Resource Selection and Maintenance Policy," http://gailborden.info/about-the-library/library-policies/1270-resource-selection-and-maintenance-policy.
29. Midlothian Public Library, "Programming Policy," www.midlothianlibrary.org/sitemedia/PDF/Policies/ProgrammingPolicy20182.pdf.
30. Wells Public Library, "Programming Policy," www.wellslibrary.org/ckfinder/userfiles/files/Programming%20Policy%20with%202016%20Revisions(1).PDF.
31. Gail Borden Public Library District, "Librarians vs. Fake News," http://gailborden.info/fakenews.
32. Portland Public Library, "Civic Saturday," https://www.portlandlibrary.com/events/civic-saturday.

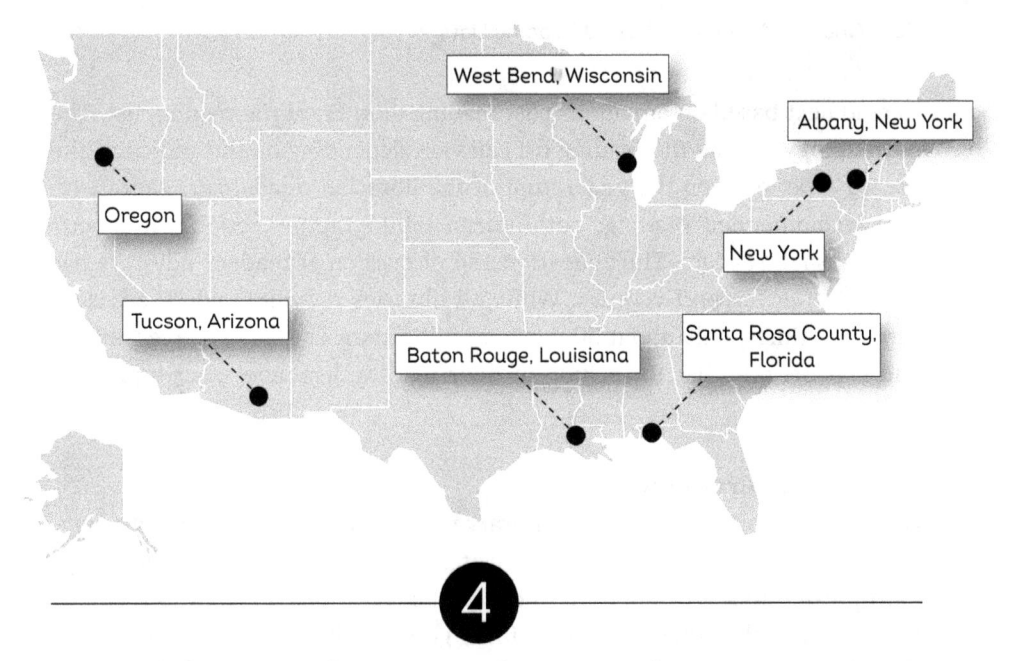

Map locations: Oregon; West Bend, Wisconsin; Albany, New York; New York; Tucson, Arizona; Baton Rouge, Louisiana; Santa Rosa County, Florida

4

Bookmarks and Reading Lists

BOTH THE MAGIC OF STORIES AND THE GUIDANCE OF LIBRARIANS are boundless. And when these are combined, hungry readers can travel the universe. But the universe is a big place filled with thousands of libraries and millions of books. That's why the guidance of the librarian is so important. Linton Weeks said, "In the nonstop tsunami of global information, librarians provide us with floaties and teach us to swim."

What to Read Next

The motivation behind every librarian's actions is a sincere desire to connect a person with a resource that enriches his or her life. The people, the institution, and the resource are all just details. It's all about connection. *Readers' advisory* is an industry term for that connection, and is usually used with regard to adult fiction readers. Joyce Saricks, the author of *Readers' Advisory Service in the Public Library,* defines the concept: readers' advisory "is a patron-centered library service for adult leisure readers. A successful readers' advisory service is one in which knowledgeable, nonjudgmental staff help fiction and nonfiction readers with their leisure-reading needs."[1]

Librarians know that they can't interact with every person who walks through the door, so they've embraced other means of sharing ideas for what to read next based on a reader's past reading diet. Enter the reading list. The terminology around the reading list can vary depending on the audience, the library type, or even the generation of the librarian: readalikes, genreflecting, recommended reading, pathfinders, bibliographies, book talks, book trailers, shelf readers. The education and discussion of readers' advisory has fluctuated in the past century. While all libraries provide readers' advisory service at times, only about 50 percent of librarians actually receive training and support on what to include in their reading lists and what topics are off-limits.

Direct or Indirect Means

Other than a conversation with a library worker, browsing the library's pamphlet area, or visiting the library website, the average person is going to be hard-pressed to know where to find expert suggestions on what to read. All they know is that they're looking for a good book, and who better to ask than the person who works with books all day? There's an assumed love and knowledge of books ingrained in the stereotype of librarians. But in many cases, this isn't a stereotype; many librarians have a passion for sharing the love of reading, and they love to share books that others might love too.

In the absence of a one-on-one conversation or a readers' advisory interview with book seekers, librarians use both print and digital methods for sharing recommendations. Librarians have often created paper bookmarks, with reading lists based on topics or pamphlets that highlight an author and other books that read like theirs. Libraries might have drop-down menus on their website that focus on traditional genres or specific requests. Shelf talkers are an easy way to personalize book recommendations from staff the community knows and add an informal review or description of the book. Readers' advisory lists, posters, bookmarks, and shelf talkers are often sprinkled throughout the library's physical space and virtual space: not just the website, but the catalog, social media, and e-mail signatures too.

DIRECTIONAL AIDS

Illustrated posters of award winners and creative directional aids to suggest topics and titles are also ways of suggesting books that may be of interest to readers. Sometimes publishers will put together downloadable materials or products for purchase that highlight awards or topics of interest, and which suggest good books to read. The main goal is always to promote library use, reading, and knowledge.

CRITERIA
The criteria for suggesting resources to individuals or for recommending something worth reading to a student who is seeking leisure reading are different from selecting material for a class or group, just as they differ from the criteria used for selecting materials for a library collection. But the librarian selects, not censors, books. Selection implies that a librarian or educator is free to choose this or that work, depending on the purpose to be achieved and the recipient in question. Censorship, by contrast, implies that certain works are simply not open to selection, whatever the circumstances.

AUTHORITY AND EXPERTISE
Posters, bookmarks, websites, and shelf talkers are just formats in which a reading list is displayed. The intent and authority behind the reading list are actually its distinguishing characteristics. Reading lists are often implemented by schools and extracurricular programs. Whereas a public librarian might create a list to highlight a *New York Times* best-selling novel and suggest other titles like it, a school librarian might create a list of books that expose students to a 1920s setting, in order to accompany a teacher's study of Prohibition. If the assignment is to read a book from the list, is the list part of the curriculum? Does the authority lie with the teacher or with the librarian? And if there is a complaint, is the topic of the booklist the problem, or is it the specific title? If a book is removed from a list because of a complaint, is that censorship? If the list is removed altogether, is that censorship?

Arguable Advisory

Very seldom is there an ulterior motive for creating lists of suggested readings or guiding the pursuit of knowledge. But there have been many times when a librarian's agenda has been criticized by outsiders and the whole list is called into question.

West Bend, Wisconsin
In 2009, a patron of the West Bend Community Memorial Library delivered a written letter of complaint through the library's book drop about a list of YA books on the website that had LGBTQ characters and content. The list had been created in collaboration with the local high school's Gay Straight Alliance (GSA) by the young adult librarian. The list had been published on the

48 | Chapter 4: Bookmarks and Reading Lists

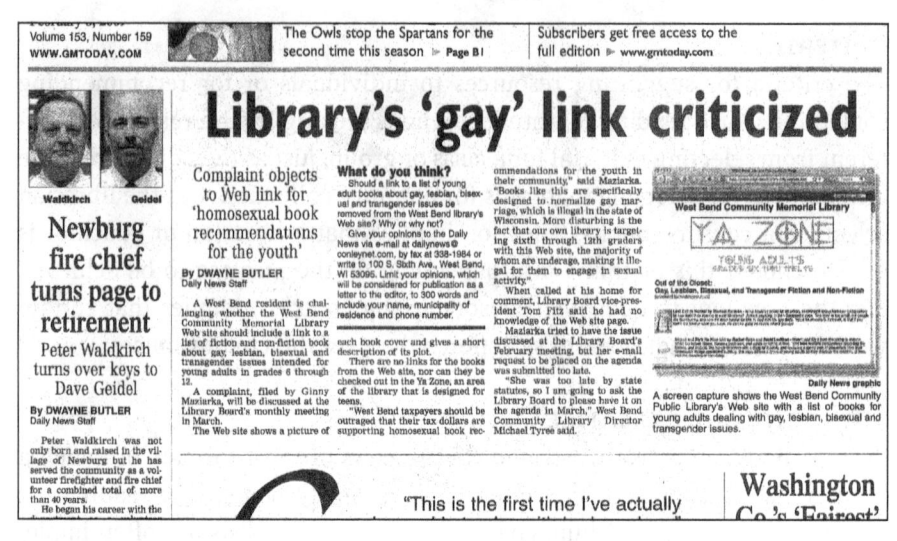

FIGURE 4.1 *West Bend Daily News* front page

library's website for five years before the complaint surfaced. Days after the complaint was issued, the town newspaper led with the headline "Library's 'Gay' Link Criticized."

When the community member found no avenue for protesting the existence of the readers' advisory list, her demand shifted from removing the list from the website to removing all of the books on the list from the library. The first formal reconsideration form listed thirty-seven books, including *The Perks of Being a Wallflower* by Stephen Chbosky, *Geography Club* by Brent Hartinger, and many others that would be censored for being "gay propaganda" and "sexually explicit."[2]

Acting in accordance with the library's policy, the complainants met with the YA librarian and the library director. No resolution could be found, so the appeal was scheduled to go before the library board. The first of multiple attempts to hold the library's monthly board meetings was subsequently postponed by the fire department because the number of people in attendance exceeded the room's capacity limit of 265 people. Frustrated by the delay, the complainants hosted their own town hall meeting where minors were prohibited. A petition was circulated with five demands, including the "Reclassification of Youth-Targeted Pornographic Books into the Adult Section of the Library."[3] The petition also demanded that the library balance its shelves with books "affirming traditional heterosexual perspectives" that are faith-based or written by "ex-gay" authors.

During the next month's local spring elections, the West Bend City Council got involved and refused to reappoint four library board members that it deemed unqualified: an attorney, a high school teacher, an elementary school librarian, and a retired teacher and bookstore employee. In the agitation over the issue, multiple organizations were created and vocal community members blogged, wrote to the newspaper, gathered petition signatures, and recruited support for their point of view.

Every e-mail, letter, and video was documented with open records requests and blog entries. After six months of emotional attacks and national news reports, the West Bend Community Memorial Library Board held their meeting in an elementary school gymnasium where hundreds attended and sixty people spoke their opinions. The final votes were cast unanimously (by the original board members who were serving the reminder of their terms) to retain all eighty-two books in the library, and even the teen readers' advisory website stayed.[4]

Oregon Battle of the Books

The entire state of Oregon participates in an annual voluntary reading program for students which is sponsored by the Oregon Association of School Librarians. The Oregon Battle of the Books (OBOB) is promoted through school districts around the state, and school librarians volunteer to serve on a committee that chooses the books on the list each year.[5] The 2018–2019 book list for 3rd – 5th grade competitors included an award-winning middle grade novel, *George*, by Alex Gino, with a transgender girl as the main character.

Many parents took issue with the selection, and consequently a few school districts dropped out from the program, thus prohibiting any of their students from participating in it.[6] The districts' public statements cited the book's content as the reason for withdrawing, saying, for example, that "it didn't align with the district health curriculum."

The conservative group Parents' Rights in Education adopted the statewide controversy to further its platform against transgender rights by suggesting that "a reading list including stories about transgender people cause children to question their gender identities for attention."[7]

After parents launched an online petition to remove *George*, the Lake Oswego School District superintendent wrote that his district would remain a participant in OBOB: "Our students have a choice whether or not to participate in OBOB. If they choose to participate, students will read from the entire list, not an edited list."[8] The OBOB committee and associated organizations kept the 2018–2019 book list intact.

Albany, New York

For many people, asking for help is hard enough, even if it's just asking a librarian where to find a certain topic of books. When patrons are looking for sensitive materials like teen pregnancy or bulimia, they often wonder, "What if the librarian knows me or knows my family?" or "What if she tells someone?" Librarians pride themselves on holding confidential, nonjudgmental reference interviews, but the patrons may not know that. In Albany and many other cities and towns across the country, compassionate librarians who want to provide a service for teens (and adults) who may be unable or unwilling to ask for help have crafted a broad list of tough topics with their corresponding Dewey Decimal call numbers. The lists of topics are offered as bookmarks or posters as an indirect means of guiding patrons to information.

A parent at the Albany Public Library complained about the library's list, saying that the library shouldn't be encouraging kids to look up this type of information.[9] It's not uncommon for embarrassment or fear to prompt kids to steal or hide books about depression, divorce, or sexually transmitted diseases rather than ask for help. The librarians at Albany have stated that the value of helping teens who need those resources outweighs any complaints about them. They've agreed that the posters will not be removed.

New York

For a school district in New York State, a new school librarian compiled a summer reading list for sixth-graders at the request of her principal. She asked the teachers and principal for input on the list. Upon receiving no edits or concerns, the principal circulated the list to families.

When a parent vocalized a strong objection to the inclusion of Lisa Bunker's science-fiction novel *Felix Yz* on the list, the principal not only e-mailed the families to pull the reading list, but the librarian was subjected to disciplinary action and was ultimately terminated. No formal review process was implemented.

Santa Rosa County, Florida

Every year, Jay High School in Santa Rosa County participates in Celebrate Literacy Week along with other high schools in the state, with each district scheduling different literacy programs and projects. The January occasion is organized by the Florida Department of Education with the goal of promoting literacy and excellent reading habits in the students of Florida.

Jay High School chose to do a school-wide read during the 2017 Celebrate Literacy Week with a book chosen by the high school teachers: *Gutless* by Carl Deuker, a coming-of-age novel about a high school quarterback that explores themes of bullying, friendship, and abuse of power. According to the district's plans, "students will learn how to change the world through the character education lessons learned by the novel's protagonist." After the close of Celebrate Literacy Week, the students would get to skype with the author.[10]

Before the students could meet the author, though, some parents objected to portions of the book that they felt were inappropriate, and they complained to the administrators. Santa Rosa County's director of high schools, Jason Weeks, Jay High School's principal, Stephen Knowlton, and Superintendent Tim Wyrosdick agreed with the parents' assessment of the content and pulled the book.

To the *Santa Rosa's Press Gazette*, Weeks said: "It's more about body parts, and things like that that shouldn't be discussed; it's inappropriate in that nature." Because this decision didn't impact the library or curriculum, administrators judged that no formal review process was necessary.[11]

When the book's author, Carl Deuker, was interviewed, he said: "By objecting to a passage taken out of context, the parents who got *Gutless* banned provide a classic example to their young adult children of how not to read. Even more disturbing is that both the principal and the superintendent buckled to the protest."[12]

Baton Rouge, Louisiana

The Louisiana Teen Readers' Choice program provides a recreational reading list for teens. Organized by the Louisiana Center for the Book in the State Library of Louisiana, the list's purpose is to foster a love of reading in teens by encouraging them to vote on outstanding books. A committee of Louisiana librarians and educators compile the 9th–12th grade list of nominated titles. The book that receives the most votes from the students wins the honor of being the Teen Readers' Choice.

In 2014, when John Corey Whaley's Printz award-winning novel, *Where Things Come Back*, was considered out of 50 titles to be one of the 10 nominated books[13] that the teens would read and vote on, there was contention within the committee. Three YA librarian members of the Louisiana Teen Readers' Choice committee resigned over the decision to include *Where Things Come Back* on the 2014 list.

Whaley is a Louisiana native, and his book was the winner of both the Printz Award and the Morris Award in 2012, so it was an obvious choice for the list. But the three librarians not only resigned from the committee, they refused to purchase it for their libraries, they discouraged others from selecting the book for their libraries, and they stopped promoting the Louisiana Teen Readers' Choice program entirely. Their concern was that the book's content was too mature for high school students and that one character in it has a crisis of faith. While the book was included in the list of ten nominated titles that the teens could choose from, it did not win the Louisiana Teen Readers' Choice award.

Tucson, Arizona

For over ten years, the Tucson Unified School District (TUSD) had been offering classes and resources as part of a specialized Mexican American Studies (MAS) program when the latter was banned by a state law passed in 2010.[14] The voluntary K–12 curriculum lists in art, government, history, and literature focused on historic and contemporary Mexican American resources. The curriculum was seen as a way to help Hispanic students see themselves, their family, and their community in their studies. Students who participated in the program showed higher test scores and graduation and attendance rates than similar peers who did not participate.

Arizona House Bill 2281, which was signed into state law by Governor Jan Brewer in 2010, made it illegal for schools to teach classes that are intended for any given ethnic group to go against another ethnic group, or advocate the overthrow of the government of the United States. The following books were not allowed to be taught in classes due to HB 2281; *500 Years of Chicano History in Pictures* by Elizabeth Martinez; *Critical Race Theory* by Richard Delgado; *Message to Aztlán: Selected Writings of Rodolfo "Corky" Gonzalez* by Rodolfo Gonzales; *Chicano! The History of the Mexican American Civil Rights Movement* by Arturo Rosales; *Rethinking Columbus* by

FIGURE 4.2 Books Banned by Arizona HB2281

Bill Bigelow and Bob Peterson; *Pedagogy of the Oppressed* by Paulo Freire; *The History of the Mexican American Civil Rights Movement* by Arturo Rosales; and *Mexican WhiteBoy* by Matt de la Peña. These books were banned because of their alleged radically anti-American worldviews and their generally racist sentiment against Americans of white European heritage.

After the bill was signed, 150 protesters walked from TUSD headquarters to the Arizona state building. When the building was due to close, fifteen people, including students, sat down on a second-floor balcony and refused to leave. They were arrested and cited with trespassing.[15] Facing the loss of 10 percent of their budget if they failed to comply—some $14 million over the fiscal year—Tucson's school board voted to shut the MAS classes down in January 2011.

The elimination of the program led to the removal of hundreds of books from TUSD school libraries, including works by Isabel Allende, Junot Díaz, Dagoberto Gilb, Howard Zinn, Henry David Thoreau, and even William Shakespeare.[16] The books used in the program were collected from students and placed in boxes marked "banned." Former teachers of the program and students filed lawsuits to dispute the bill's constitutionality; *Arce v. Douglas* (formerly *Arce v. Huppenthal*) was originally filed on October 18, 2010, by ten teachers and the director of TUSD's MAS program.[17]

The Librotraficantes (Spanish for "book smugglers"), a group founded in 2012 to protest the elimination of the Tucson program, traveled more than 1,000 miles from Houston, carrying books from the forbidden program to establish underground libraries in several cities. The American Library Association passed a resolution at its 2012 Midwinter Meeting opposing the state's new restrictions.[18]

In late 2013 First Amendment groups, including the Freedom to Read Foundation, filed an amicus brief in *Arce v. Huppenthal*, a lawsuit challenging the constitutionality of Arizona HB 2281. "In submitting this brief, the Freedom to Read Foundation is standing up for the right of all Arizona students to a curriculum based on educational merit, not political motivation," said Executive Director Barbara M. Jones.[19]

In 2017, a federal judge ruled that the law used to ban Mexican American studies from the public secondary school curriculum had been both created and enforced with anti-Mexican American racial animus. While the law was deemed unconstitutional, the Tucson Unified School District is dragging its heels at re-implementing any of the resources from the Mexican American Studies curriculum.[20]

The Right to Suggest, Engage, and Teach

The First Amendment protects the right to receive information. Receiving information is often precipitated by an educator offering suggestions, engaging students' interest, or igniting their desire to know more. Many experiences of searching for information or pleasure reading are not solo excursions; they involve guidance from teachers.

Most academic, public, school, and special librarians have had to guide users through a learning process. Whether it is showing a user how to download an app on a tablet or smartphone, reserve a book through the catalog, or access and use a library database, these services are second nature to librarians' work with the people who use the facility. Additionally, programs and classes offer a variety of learning opportunities: help with résumés, building a website, and safeguarding social media privacy. Librarians and library staff are undoubtedly the link that brings many resources and skills to patrons. Marketing, physical location, and well-designed websites play an enormous part in raising users' awareness and interest, but many other users will not venture towards the unknown without a guide. And that guidance, or instruction, is teaching.

The majority of librarians don't have formal training in education, pedagogy, or instructional design. They seek to fill in their knowledge gaps with continuing education, seeking ways to improve their skills so that those they serve get the most out of what they're offering.

As librarians stand to protect the First Amendment freedoms of access, exploration, and reading for their community, it is implicit that there should also be protected freedoms for the professional duty of providing those resources and guiding users to expand their knowledge and skills.

Under the rights conceptualized in academic freedom, teachers in public institutions have limited freedoms to teach without undue restrictions. These freedoms are based on the rights to freedom of expression under the First Amendment of the Bill of Rights. The subjects taught are limited to the institution's mission and the policies that govern how these selections are made. An educator cannot be seen as promoting a personal or political agenda in the exercise of teaching or guiding instruction.

While the term *academic freedom* is usually reserved for higher education, universities, and occasionally K–12 educators, it's important to remember that traditional faculty are not the only ones who teach. While the traditional educators in a school or institution are the teachers or professors, there are many others who help instruct, educate, and guide, including librarians.

Respecting and Harnessing Professional Freedoms

ALA President Barbara Stripling said it best in the "Declaration for the Right to Libraries":

> In addition to a vast array of books, computers and other resources, library users benefit from the expert teaching and guidance of librarians and library staff to help expand their minds and open new worlds. We declare and affirm our right to quality libraries—public, school, academic, and special.[21]

It is time, well past time, that we advocate not only for the right to libraries, but for the rights of librarians to provide the expert teaching and guidance needed to expand minds and open new worlds. Quality libraries are quality libraries because of the librarians who strive for excellence in readers' advisory, the cultivation of superior book lists, and the recommendation of engaging resources to develop thoughtful citizens in our democracy.

In 2019, the ALA Council adopted a revised interpretation of the *Library Bill of Rights* titled "Education and Information Literacy" that strongly reinforces the role of librarians as educators. (See "Education and Information Literacy" and other interpretations of the *Library Bill of Rights* in the Appendix.) Libraries and library workers foster education by promoting the free expression and interchange of diverse ideas, leading to lifelong learners. Libraries use resources, programming, and services to strengthen access to information and thus build a foundation of intellectual freedom. In their roles as educators, library workers create an environment that nurtures intellectual freedom in all library resources and services.[22]

Libraries, schools, and universities wishing to foster intellectual freedom should create an environment in which their professionals are encouraged to promote the free flow of a wide range of perspectives, while also creating an environment that is safe for a diverse group of students and users. Such an environment is codified by formal policies and procedures that protect the staff who guide and instruct students and other users.

There are a number of practical ways that administrators can support the creative and educational pursuits of librarians to advocate for library use, lifelong learning, and a passion for reading:

- Exemplify dialogue and discussion that acknowledges staff skills and encourages their ambition towards excellence.
- Devote time at staff meetings to sharing stories of excellent service and instruction.
- Routinely highlight the new ideas and initiatives of colleagues to other staff and stakeholders.
- Provide opportunities and financing for professional development and continuing education.
- Outline clear guidance, education, resources, and expectations to support staff in their responsibilities.
- Protect the integrity of librarians' work and reputation in defending the intellectual freedom of students and library users.
- Recognize the privilege and power of leadership.
- Establish clear channels of communication in expressing new ideas or concerns.

- Engage library users, stakeholders, and the community in the strong support of intellectual freedom and respect for the professional skills of library staff and educators.

The ALA's *Code of Ethics* states: "We strive for excellence in the profession by maintaining and enhancing our own knowledge and skills, by encouraging the professional development of co-workers, and by fostering the aspirations of potential members of the profession."[23]

The Buck Stops Here

Ultimately, the responsibility for the work environment lies with those in power who are charged with implementing policy. The value placed on the professional skills of librarians needs to come from within the heart of the institution. Associations and professional development can advocate for the ethical obligation to nourish intellectual and academic freedom, but those values need to be reflected locally.

If a library or public institution claims to value intellectual and academic freedom for its professionals, then the following ideals of academic freedom should be embraced:[24]

- Academic freedom means that librarians, staff, and users can engage in intellectual conversations without fear of censorship or retaliation.
- Academic freedom does not mean a library worker can harass, threaten, intimidate, ridicule, or impose his or her views on others.
- Academic freedom gives both library workers and users the right to express their views—in speech and writing—without fear of punishment, unless the means of expression substantially hinders the rights of others or, in the case of librarians, those views demonstrate that they are professionally ignorant, incompetent, or dishonest with regard to their discipline or fields of expertise.
- Academic freedom means that the political, religious, or philosophical beliefs of politicians, administrators, and members of the public cannot be imposed on library staff or patrons.
- Academic freedom gives library workers the right to seek redress if they believe their rights have been violated.
- Academic freedom protects library workers and users from reprisals for respectfully disagreeing with administrative policies or proposals.

- Academic freedom does not exclude library staff from following an institution's required policies and procedures.
- Academic freedom gives library staff and users the right to challenge one another's views, but not to penalize them for holding them.
- Academic freedom gives librarians substantial latitude in deciding how to instruct, design, guide and facilitate the tasks for which they are responsible.
- Academic freedom does not protect against complaints about the content or manner of providing library service or materials.
- Academic freedom does not protect an incompetent library worker from losing his or her job. Academic freedom does not grant lifetime employment.
- Academic freedom does not protect library staff from noninstitutional penalties if they break the law.
- Academic freedom does not protect library workers from disciplinary action, but it does require that they receive fair treatment and due process.

Academic freedoms help libraries and schools fulfill their mission of imparting knowledge and encouraging academic excellence. But academic freedom is a privilege and not a guarantee.

Consequences of the Pipeline

In 1951, in the case of *Adler v. Board of Education*, Justice William O. Douglas wrote:

> Where suspicion fills the air and holds scholars in line for fear of their jobs, there can be no exercise of the free intellect . . . A problem can no longer be pursued with impunity to its edges. Fear stalks the classroom. the teacher is no longer a stimulant to adventurous thinking; she becomes instead a pipe line for safe and sound information. A deadening dogma takes the place of free inquiry. Instruction tends to become sterile; pursuit of knowledge is discouraged; discussion often leaves off where it should begin.[25]

Pipes sink, they rust, they get clogged. Pipes break, and freeze, and burst. Our society needs the passion to explore, to think, to read and to travel the universe with expert guides.

NOTES

1. Joyce G. Saricks, *Readers' Advisory Service in the Public Library* (Chicago: American Library Association, 2005).
2. Jason Hanna, "Library Fight Riles Up City, Leads to Book-Burning Demand," CNN, July 22, 2009, www.cnn.com/2009/US/07/22/wisconsin.book.row/index.html.
3. Michael Zimmer, "West Bend Library Controversy Continues to Escalate," *Michaelzimmer.org* (blog), June 16, 2009, https://www.michaelzimmer.org/2009/06/16/west-bend-library-controversy-continues-to-escalate.
4. *Library Service to GLBTQ Teens* (blog), "Evolution of a Real-Life GLBTQ Materials Challenge: The West Bend Story," http://glbtqinthelibrary.weebly.com/evolution-of-a-challenge—-the-west-bend-story.html; Don Behm, "Library Board Rejects Restrictions," *Journal Sentinel*, June 2, 2009, http://archive.jsonline.com/news/wisconsin/46772872.html.
5. Oregon Battle of the Books, www.oregonbattleofthebooks.org.
6. Sarah Lorge Butler, "Parents Are Divided over a Book in a Popular Student Reading Program in Oregon," *New York Times*, May 8, 2018, https://www.nytimes.com/2018/05/08/books/george-alex-gino-controversy-oregon.html.
7. April Baer, "Book about Transgender Girl Breaks Ground—And Stirs Controversy—In Oregon Schools," Oregon Public Broadcasting, May 19, 2018, https://www.opb.org/news/article/george-book-transgender-girl-oregon-battle-district/.
8. Claire Holley, "Lake Oswego School District Stands Behind Book at Center of State 'Battle,'" *Lake Oswego Review*, May 16, 2018, https://portlandtribune.com/lor/108-education/395774-288821-lake-oswego-school-district-stands-behind-book-at-center-of-state-battle.
9. Anny McCloy, "Library Says Controversial Poster Won't Come Down, Even after Parent Complaints," CBS6 Albany, November 11, 2017, https://cbs6albany.com/news/local/only-on-6-library-says-controversial-poster-wont-come-down-even-after-parent-complaints.
10. Florida Department of Education, "Celebrate Literacy Week," www.fldoe.org/core/fileparse.php/7540/urlt/clw17-SantaRosa.pdf.
11. Aaron Little, "Jay High Bans Book from Celebrate Literacy Week," *Santa Rosa's Press Gazette*, February 2, 2017, www.srpressgazette.com/news/20170202/jay-high-bans-book-from-celebrate-literacy-week.

12. Jillian Kay Melchior, "IRONY ALERT: Florida School Yanks Controversial Book during 'Celebrate Literacy Week,'" *Heat Street*, February 15, 2017, http://iwf.org/news/2802847/IRONY-ALERT:-Florida-School-Yanks-Controversial-Book-During-%E2%80%98Celebrate-Literacy-Week%E2%80%99.
13. Louisiana Library Association, "2014 Louisiana Teen Readers' Choice Award Recipients," http://ltrc.state.lib.la.us/2014/books.php.
14. CNN Wire Staff, "Arizona Limits Ethnic Studies in Public Schools," CNN, May 13, 2010, www.cnn.com/2010/POLITICS/05/12/arizona.ethnic.studies/index.html.
15. Dylan Smith, "15 Arrested after Horne Press Conference on Ethnic Studies Ban," *Tucson Sentinel*, May 12, 2010, www.tucsonsentinel.com/local/report/051210_horne_sitin/15-arrested-after-horne-press-conference-ethnic-studies-ban.
16. Phil Morehart, "A Year in the Life of Librotraficante," *American Libraries*, May 14, 2013, https://americanlibrariesmagazine.org/2013/05/14/a-year-in-the-life-of-librotraficante.
17. Nanette Perez, "Resolution Opposing Restriction of Access to Materials and Open Inquiry in Ethnic and Cultural Studies Programs in Arizona," *Intellectual Freedom* (blog), January 24, 2012, https://www.oif.ala.org/oif/?p=3157.
18. Perez, "Resolution Opposing Restriction of Access to Materials," https://www.oif.ala.org/oif/?p=3157.
19. Jonathan Kelley, "Freedom to Read Foundation Files Brief in Lawsuit Challenging Arizona's Ethnic Studies Ban," Freedom to Read Foundation, November 26, 2013, https://www.ftrf.org/news/news.asp?id=148305.
20. Hank Stephenson, "TUSD Board Majority Sidesteps Effort to Resurrect Aspects of Mexican American Studies," Tucson.com, January 31, 2018, https://tucson.com/news/local/tusd-board-majority-sidesteps-effort-to-resurrect-aspects-of-mexican/article_620f0e1b-6b09-57c3-ae4c-342130d3b612.html.
21. American Library Association, "Declaration for the Right to Libraries," www.ala.org/advocacy/declaration-right-libraries.
22. American Library Association, "Education and Information Literacy," www.ala.org/advocacy/intfreedom/librarybill/interpretations/education.
23. American Library Association, "Professional Ethics," www.ala.org/tools/ethics.
24. Cary Nelson, "Defining Academic Freedom," *Inside Higher Ed*, December 21, 2010, https://www.insidehighered.com/views/2010/12/21/defining-academic-freedom.
25. *Adler v. Board of Education of City of New York*, 342 U.S. 485 (1952).

5

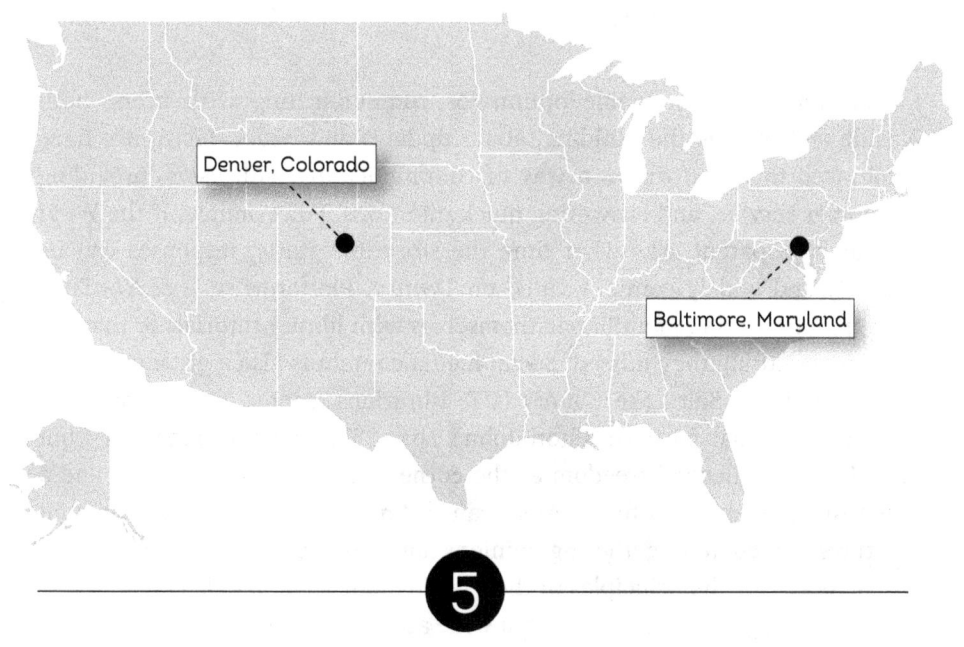

Social Media

***FORBES* MAGAZINE RECOGNIZED KIM GARST AS ONE OF THE TOP** ten power influences in social media. Garst is often quoted as saying that "conversations are happening whether you are there or not." Communities, large and small, are abundant with social media groups and pages that provide the resources people want and events that people are attending. Librarians, as part of these communities and active within these social media groups can reach large audiences of social media users, as well as use social media to discover where their audience is.

Community Communication

Libraries now use social media to do so many things: they document their successes and promote access; and perhaps most importantly, they notify social media users when new books arrive, an author visits students, the book club meets, a new book display is set up, the makerspace is in session, or a building project is complete. Engaging frequent users and enticing new users is the number-one motivation for investing time and effort on the relatively new endeavor of social media. Whether it's Twitter, Facebook, Instagram, or YouTube, librarians are harnessing their virtual powers and social reach to inform and engage their communities.

Twitter can be a viable option for communicating with users, both inside and outside the building, about updates and issues. Librarians have embraced this platform as a way of communicating with users, providing customer service, and answering quick questions. For example, if the Wi-Fi is out or a parent asks what time the storytime starts, responses can be quickly and widely communicated on Twitter. Platforms such as YouTube are great for users to familiarize themselves with library tutorials or to catch up on something they missed. Social media content is also a great outlet for staff creativity. Salt Lake County (UT) librarians created an extraordinary music video that parodies Elton John's song "Philadelphia Freedom," but highlights intellectual freedom as the cornerstone of library services and a First Amendment right for all Americans.[1] Whether libraries are sharing out pictures and content, gathering opinions and comments, or creating content to advocate for the principles of their profession, social media can be a successful strategy for engaging with a wide audience of users.

Social media dates back over twenty years. And while a few libraries have been using it since day one, most libraries are still relatively new to the vast possibilities and explosive growth of this media form. In 2014 the Taylor & Francis Group[2] studied the use of social media in libraries and noted that

- over 70 percent of libraries are using social media tools
- 60 percent have had a social media account for three years or longer
- 30 percent of librarians are posting at least daily
- 75 percent of libraries schedule posts on an ad hoc basis

Social media can be used to market the library, its resources, and its professional staff and their skills to community members and colleagues. Sharing student projects and innovations on social media will empower students' voices.

All types of libraries and a wide variety of professional and front-line staff manage and create content for social media platforms. Staff can promote books and resources in creative ways or attempt to poll their followers on what materials are popular and most needed. New books, articles, and blogs are publishing best practices, marketing and imaging tools, and are researching the use and return on effort on social media. There are even entire library positions created to capitalize on the skills and experience of librarians who are talented in the art of using social media for marketing purposes.

As the technology develops and more and more librarians are gaining professional training and experience in social media marketing and digital curation, the resources being published on this field also increase. But whether they are technology reports or marketing tips, these resources—a snapshot of what is being published—lack necessary information about managing controversies and the obligations of public institutions. The following is a list of sources on how libraries can use social media:

- *Doing Social Media So It Matters: A Librarian's Guide*, by Laura Solomon (American Library Association, 2011)
- *Google This! Putting Google and Other Social Media Sites to Work for Your Library*, by Terry Ballard (Chandos, 2012)
- *Managing Your Library's Social Media Channels*, by David Lee King (American Library Association, 2015)
- *Marketing and Social Media: A Guide for Libraries, Archives, and Museums*, by Christie Koontz (Rowman and Littlefield, 2014)
- *Marketing with Social Media: A LITA Guide*, by Beth C. Thomsett-Scott (ALA Neal-Schuman, 2018)
- *Social Media Curation*, by Joyce Valenza (ALA TechSource, 2014)
- *Social Media for Academics: A Practical Guide*, by Diane Rasmussen Neal (Chandos, 2012)
- *Social Media for Creative Libraries*, by Phil Bradley (Facet, 2015)
- *Social Media Optimization: Principles for Building and Engaging Community*, by Scott W. H. Young and Doralyn Rossmann (ALA TechSource, 2016)
- *Successful Social Networking in Public Libraries*, by Walt Crawford (American Library Association, 2012)
- *The Librarian's Nitty-Gritty Guide to Social Media*, by Laura Solomon (American Library Association, 2013)
- *Using Social Media to Build Library Communities: A LITA Guide*, by Scott W. H. Young and Doralyn Rossmann, eds. (Rowman and Littlefield, 2017)

Unfortunately, barely more than a paragraph in any of these books is devoted to the potential problems and pitfalls associated with creating content on social media. There's no mention of how to address complaints or challenges to online posts or tweets. In this relatively new world of professional marketing librarians, we need to fully prepare for controversy and public relations crises. As Benjamin Franklin said: "By failing to prepare, you are preparing to fail."

Many of the controversies surrounding libraries and social media involve an employee expressing personal opinions online that are found to be detrimental to the library's reputation or not in alignment with the library's policies or mission. This chapter's focus, however, is on social media content that is created by librarians or shared on library platforms that falls within the professional capacity of their social media mission. In addition to library-initiated content, there needs to be more attention to the First Amendment protection of how online communities communicate with their representatives and government agencies, which include many publicly funded libraries.

In order to fully embrace the concept of community communication as a two-way street, there needs to be a higher expectation that government officials and public employees cannot delete legitimate concerns and opinions that are reasonably expressed and protected by the First Amendment.

Libraries use social media to build their brand as an active voice in a community, school, corporation, or university. Building this reputation within a thriving environment is essential to success, but it is not without some risks. When libraries establish their social media platforms as an avenue of communication, they are creating a limited public forum where speech, and even criticisms, are protected by the First Amendment.

Tarnished Tweets

Social media censorship isn't common. Or at least it isn't reported. It is more likely that a librarian will delete a comment or block a user, than to have a complaint come up about content that was created by staff and posted on the library's social media accounts. As the legalities of free speech on social media platforms, like Twitter and Facebook, are getting ironed out (and sometimes are changing daily), the fact is that public institutions are still public and are held responsible to their taxpayers.

Denver, Colorado

The Jefferson County Public Library deleted more than a dozen of its Twitter posts after Commissioner Don Rosier relayed a constituent's concerns that the library's social media account was politically biased.[3] Rosier said he was

FIGURE 5.1 Jefferson County Library tweets

"shocked and appalled" by the tweets in question, which he described as promoting a "one-sided political view."[4] In a press e-mail, Pam Nissler, the library director, wrote: "We would never want to be perceived as taking sides, or promoting a particular point of view. In this case, I felt that our postings created the perception of bias and I removed them." James LaRue, director of the ALA's Office for Intellectual Freedom, weighed in on this issue, stating that he "did not find anything objectionable to [the tweets]." He said the tweets were only reflecting current societal topics and did not push a certain political viewpoint.

Baltimore, Maryland

In their efforts to raise awareness of Banned Books Week, some libraries, schools, and universities use a police lineup background and post pictures of a person reading banned or challenged books with props such as a mug-shot letter board that says "Caught Reading a Banned Book" or "Rebel Reader." Some libraries have even dramatized the issue by creating "jails" or having local law enforcement "arrest" library staff. These ideas and visual representations start conversations around the historic legality of reading, the difference between the United States' First Amendment protections and the laws in other countries that do criminalize certain viewpoints, and the dangers of only a few people deciding what is permissible for the majority of people to read.

For Banned Books Week, the Enoch Pratt Free Library crafted a mock mug-shot backdrop where pictures could be taken to celebrate the freedom to read.[5] After pictures were posted on the library's social media accounts with the text, "We have #rebelreaders at the Edmondson Avenue Branch. What are you reading during #BannedBooksWeek?" several comments criticized the library for including African American students in the mug shots. Wendy O. Osefo, a political commentator and professor at Johns Hopkins University, said the library's tweets played into the "school to prison pipeline" stereotype of black people.[6]

Elected Officials and Public Agencies

The rules are still being debated in many areas of social media. The social media accounts of government agencies and public figures are particularly controversial, with consistent reports being broadcast about the different standards that people in the public sector are held to when they are online.

In Vermont, Washington, Nebraska, Maryland, Maine, and Kentucky,[7] ACLU chapters are suing elected officials for blocking their constituents on social media. "Blocking someone from viewing public information on a government-operated social media page is a clear violation of the First Amendment." In some cases, citizens were blocked or their posts were deleted because they expressed displeasure with voting decisions. And in other cases, walls were wiped of any critical comments.

In its letters, the ACLU describes the social media pages of elected officials and public agencies as "limited public forums" protected by the First Amendment. It says that lawmakers can regulate speech such as vulgar or off-topic posts on those forums, "but viewpoint discrimination—for example, removing posts or blocking particular users entirely on the basis of the point of view expressed—is never permissible since it violates the First Amendment right to free speech."[8]

On July 25, 2017, Senior Judge James C. Cacheris for the Eastern District of Virginia ruled that Phyllis J. Randall, the chair of the Loudoun County Board of Supervisors, took part in viewpoint discrimination. Randall had blocked Brian C. Davison from commenting on her Facebook page after Davison posted a comment alleging that Loudoun County's school board was corrupt. Randall soon reinstated Davison but Davison sued, alleging a First Amendment violation by Randall.[9]

Johannesburg, South Africa

Schools and libraries not only use social media to promote events, but often share pictures with their followers of events that they've recently hosted. People enjoy seeing pictures of themselves and their families and neighbors at these events. By posting these pictures, libraries demonstrate that their events are popular and well-attended.

At Rivonia Primary School in Johannesburg, photos of the school's Fun Day Haunted House were removed from the school's Facebook page because of comments that prompted a social media group to criticize the school for "promoting violence in an already violent country."[10] There were no complaints about violence or fear from anyone who attended the event; the complaints were just about the photos posted on social media.

The Right to Post and the Right to Block

The number-one thing to remember about social media platforms is that participation on them is not a protected right. Nor is any one person or institution required to use their account as a communication path. Facebook, Twitter, YouTube, Google, and Instagram are all independently and privately owned companies. Each corporation has its own set of terms and conditions that users must agree to when creating an account. Just as publishing companies determine what books to print based on criteria crafted by the company, social media companies can specify content they will not publish on their media platforms, in alignment with the company's policies and mission. In addition, there is no obligation for the public on social media sites to publish accurate or unbiased information. The Telecommunications Act of 1996—in many ways the first law that regulated the internet—codified in law that those providing internet services are not publishers. They cannot be held responsible for content posted by third parties. Internet service providers are merely considered the means to an end.[11]

Before 1987 the U.S. government did impose a fairness requirement on broadcast media. In 1949, the Federal Communications Commission began requiring broadcasters to air both sides of controversial issues through the Fairness Doctrine. The Supreme Court later upheld the Fairness Doctrine by arguing that radio and television broadcasters had an obligation to present balanced coverage because they used the public's airwaves. Opponents of the Fairness Doctrine argued that requiring balance had dampened the ability to spread a partisan perspective or advocate for alternative ideas. When the Fairness Doctrine was repealed by the Reagan administration, it was considered by some as a victory for free speech. But in fact, it has opened the door to today's lack of regulation of social media, and their consequent factual unreliability. In any case, any effort by the government to influence or regulate what social media platforms publish risks violating the First Amendment.[12]

There are few laws[13] that address issues of copyright, privacy, and workplace speech on social media. For the most part, social media is still unregulated. Moreover, it's difficult to provide guidance in an area of law that has few precedents. Many states have enacted statutes that limit the monitoring of social media by employers; specifically, these statutes prohibit employers from demanding their employees' social media log-ins and passwords. Communication is a key component to using social media. For many users, this ease of communication is the sole purpose for social media's existence. Because of this, there has been some growth in regulation and legal precedents in the area of blocking users who are communicating specifically with elected officials and public agencies.

The ACLU argues that a government agency cannot kick a concerned constituent out of a public hearing just because he or she disagrees with an elected official. The same principles apply in a digital venue. When an elected official or government agency is using social media to communicate with the public, the government cannot pick and choose who gets to see that information and respond to it.[14] Public libraries, some of which qualify as government agencies, are also held to these standards of openness and cannot block users from participation on their social media accounts.

To support its argument, the ACLU cites the following cases:

- *Packingham v. North Carolina*, 137 S.Ct. 1730, 1735 (2017)—The U.S. Supreme Court held that a North Carolina statute that barred registered sex offenders from websites such as Facebook and LinkedIn was unconstitutional. Justice Anthony Kennedy wrote that social media enable citizens to "petition their elected representatives and otherwise engage with them in a direct manner." That process of engagement transforms otherwise private media into public forums.[15]

- *Davison v. Loudoun County Board of Supervisors*, 2017 WL 3158389 (E.D. Va. July 25, 2017)—The U.S. District Court for the Eastern District of Virginia found that the county board chair, Phyllis Randall, was acting in an official manner in communicating with her constituents on her Facebook page, which created a public forum. The court found that by engaging in viewpoint discrimination on her Facebook page, Randall violated the plaintiff's freedom of speech rights under the First Amendment and was not entitled to block the plaintiff from communication.[16]

The growing tendency of elected officials to block constituents on social media is attracting the attention of open government and civil liberty organizations. In 2017 ProPublica, an independent, nonprofit newsroom, filed public-records requests with every state's governor and twenty-two federal agencies, asking them for lists of everyone who had been blocked on their official Facebook and Twitter accounts. The responses received so far show that governors and agencies across the country have blocked at least 1,298 accounts.[17] This is unacceptable in a country that prides itself on the First Amendment. The right to petition the government is sacred.

Saving Social Media Managers

The best way to protect libraries and librarians against social media missteps is through comprehensive training, in addition to well-researched and updated policies. While the obvious route would include training the staff who manage and create social media content, it is also recommended that all staff, volunteers, and trustees receive at least some training about the library's social media goals and their role in achieving those goals. For some staff, this training may involve raising their awareness that there is a social media policy, that the policy includes restrictions on violating patron privacy, and that it prescribes certain responsibilities for ethical social media behavior on their part as members of the library team. For other staff members, it may be training about the legalities of access to social media communication and copyright knowledge. For others, it could be professional development on new social media platforms or creative design, and best practices for engaging an audience. Board members and administrators also need to be routinely updated on how social media is used in their institution. Even if a person has no knowledge or desire to learn how to "snapchat," there should still be a basic level of awareness by stakeholders in case a crisis occurs.

Opinions differ about how much centralized control a library should exert over its social media presence and posts:

> About a third of libraries responding to the Taylor & Francis survey had a [social media] policy in place, but over 40% had no plans to introduce one. There are some clear differences of opinion across librarians in how much social media can or should be centrally controlled. Some believe that representing the library as a professional function with a consistent tone is the priority, while others believe that a more human approach is important, with individual staff free to bring their own ideas and personalities to social media activities.[18]

It's understandable that different libraries and different communities have different opinions about the role of social media in the library. But with the current state of instability, factual unreliability, and unregulated speech on social media, it's too dangerous for libraries to risk their reputation and resources by adopting the so-called "human approach."

Valuable Policies

A social media policy doesn't have to be long and wordy. The point is not to cover every possible contingency, but rather to demonstrate support for the library's engagement on social media and employees' efforts to advocate for the library, literacy, and lifelong learning.

"Social media offers opportunities to connect with our users. The Cary Memorial Library uses various forms of social media and encourages staff to engage in responsible and productive online conversations." These are the opening sentences of the social media policy at the Cary Memorial Library in Lexington, Massachusetts.[19] Their policy is thorough enough to cover copyright and privacy concerns, but broad enough to allow a certain amount of creative freedom for the library's social media working group to produce and share content. The policy is current (as of September 2018) and approved by the library board, which also protects the library administration and staff when there are complaints. The Cary Memorial Library is cognizant of Massachusetts public records laws and includes a sentence in its policy that reflects their value for transparency: "Any content maintained in Library social media is a public record, including all comments and messages exchanged with Cary Memorial Library."

Many libraries have adopted social media policies that are murky at best. The questions left unanswered by many such policies include:

- Who determines if any content or comments are offensive, inappropriate, or abusive?
- How is a report made? E-mail the director? An online form? Tell the staff? Report to the social media platform?
- How long should it take to address a concern?
- Is there a recourse for a patron, student, or staff member to appeal the library's decision to remove or block a post or comment?

Pima County (AZ) offers thorough administrative guidelines for all of its government departments, which include the library, on how to manage their social media platforms. The county's guidelines clearly outline its motivation for using social media, who is responsible, and furnishes examples of types of communication to be distributed.[20] The guidelines offer a recourse for members of the public to appeal deletion of their comments, but there is still no formal recourse for expressing concern about content that library staff post.

The Kansas City Library[21] (MO) has clear social media guidelines for its employees that address not only the central location, but all the branches and departments with various social media accounts. There is a clear and positive statement in the guidelines about the library's voice as expressed by its employees:

> As you will be perceived as representing the Library whenever you post on a social network, please remember our mission statement: The Kansas City Public Library is a doorway to knowledge for all people in our community. Our attitude should always be that of a knowledgeable friend and helper. We are representatives of, for, and to the entire community, but especially the underserved, and we will always take the

extra step to show respect to every individual and his or her position and views. This will be even harder on the internet than in person and therefore means you must lift your game to that responsibility.

While the library's guidelines are internal and don't inform the public about how challenges to library content may be addressed, there is a clear statement that these platforms are not to be equated with employees' personal accounts, and so their freedom to post content is limited: "These are the Library's accounts, not yours—a supervisor may ask you to delete content such as a post, photo, link, or comment if it is in the Library's best interest to do so. Content may also be removed or edited by Public Affairs in urgent situations."

The following are some questions to consider when developing social media guidelines to empower staff while also protecting your content:

- In considering the library's social media audience, what tools are being used to identify who your visitors are?
- Are the social media platforms for various library branches branded and managed together or independently?
- What is the purpose of the posts: information, engagement, conversation, input, and so on?
- What staff members have access to the accounts? What staff are responsible for creating content? What staff are responsible for supervising the accounts?
- How do social media use analytics impact content?
- How do the social media policy or guidelines intersect with the library's communication and marketing strategy?
- What associations, agencies, or counsel are being included when vetting policies and guidelines?
- Are staff members who work with the social media platforms allowed or encouraged to take part in training and professional development opportunities?
- How and when is feedback communicated?
- Do the guidelines address the staff's own use of social media at work?
- Are staff included in crafting the guidelines? How often are the guidelines discussed with the staff? Is feedback welcome? Are there opportunities for updating the guidelines?
- What diverse perspectives are at the table when guidelines are crafted or updated?

- What is the tone of the guidelines?
- If you were to ask your staff to use three words to describe the guidelines, what would they be?

Invest Time and Finances in Training

There are many books, conferences, webinars, articles, and experts that can help libraries create guidelines and policies that both engage their community and protect the staff. These resources are widely available, but it requires administrators to invest time, staff, and money in using them wisely.

The Library Marketing and Communications Conference is designed for library employees of any level who are involved in marketing, communication, public relations, social media, and outreach in academic, public, and special libraries. The conference's 2017 keynote was "Libraries, Crises, and Social Media" from Shel Holtz, an award-winning nonprofit communications and public relations expert.[22] This address demonstrates a need in the professional field for education on some important issues that have arisen with social media.

"Social Media Guidelines for Public and Academic Libraries"

In 2018, the ALA's Intellectual Freedom Committee (IFC) published a set of guidelines[23] for creating social media policy in public and academic libraries. The "Social Media Guidelines for Public and Academic Libraries" offer specific advice on the areas of audience and reconsideration that are often neglected in library policies and procedures. With regard to audiences, the guidelines advise:

> As a best practice, the library should identify its intended audience. An academic library may limit its intended audience to university faculty, students, staff, administrators, and alumni. It can be expanded further to include specialized communities outside of the university, such as scholars within a particular discipline, or even the general public. Public libraries may identify their audience as those people residing within their official service area.

With regard to reconsideration, the guidelines advise:

> Social media policies should provide recourse for individuals to express complaints or concerns about content posted on the library's social

media. This establishes an objective and uniform framework for all involved while protecting the creative freedom and skills needed to engage library communities. The procedure for handling complaints and for reconsidering social media content should be clearly enunciated in the policy statement and applicable to everyone. The policy should stress that no posts will be removed without following the approved procedure and no content should be removed upon the authority of a single staff member or administrator.

The IFC's guidelines provide a framework for libraries that use social media to develop policies and guidelines that cover such topics as staff responsibilities, acceptable behavior, privacy, and reconsideration forms. Using recent court cases, the guidelines explicate the definition of a "public forum" as it relates to social media platforms. "There is a great need right now for guidance in balancing a library's desire to interact with their community on social media—to 'meet them where they are'—with the need to create a space where every voice can be heard," said the guidelines' coauthor, M. Teresa Doherty, the assistant head of information services and the teaching and learning librarian at Virginia Commonwealth University. "We believe that this document will help libraries create a policy to guide their social media strategy and engage with their community."

The State of the Union

In the current climate of fake news, bots, internet trolls, spam, doxing, fandom, hashtags, memes, and clickbait, it seems like every social media user is vying for the loudest megaphone and the tallest soapbox. In this environment, it's easy to lose sight of the importance and validity of a single voice. But the First Amendment protects even the quietest and loneliest voice.

In the Supreme Court's 2017 decision on *Packingham v. North Carolina*,[24] Justice Anthony Kennedy said that digital platforms "can provide perhaps the most powerful mechanisms available to a private citizen to make his or her voice heard. They allow a person with an internet connection to 'become a town crier with a voice that resonates farther than it could from any soapbox.'" Especially in our country's libraries, the majority does not trump the minority. The single voice has weight and value.

NOTES

1. Salt Lake County Library, "Intellectual Freedom—Elton John Philadelphia Freedom (Parody)," September 24, 2017, YouTube video, 3:57, https://youtu.be/7ig5ZaJD_aU.
2. Taylor & Francis Group, "Use of Social Media by the Library: Current Practices and Future Opportunities," 2014, https://librarianresources.taylorandfrancis.com/wp-content/uploads/2017/12/White-Paper-Social-Media-in-the-Library.pdf.
3. Andrew Kenney, "Tweets That Jeffco Library Deleted after an Elected Official Complained: Muslim Authors, Women's Healthcare, Hillary Clinton, Russia, Meryl Streep," Denverite, February 23, 2017, https://denverite.com/2017/02/23/jeffco-library-deletes-posts-muslim-authors-womens-healthcare-hillary-clinton-commissioners-complaint.
4. John Aguilar, "Jeffco Library Scrubs Tweets after Getting Complaints That Posts Are Politically Biased," *Denver Post*, February 23, 2017, https://www.denverpost.com/2017/02/23/jeffco-library-tweets-county-commissioner.
5. Colin Campbell, "Pratt Library Deletes, Apologizes for Tweet Posing Black Kids in Mock Mugshots for Banned Books Promotion," *Baltimore Sun*, September 26, 2017, www.baltimoresun.com/news/maryland/baltimore-city/bs-md-ci-pratt-tweet-20170926-story.html.
6. Ida Harris, "Library in Hot Water after Tweeting Fake Mugshots of Black Kids," *USA Today*, September 28, 2017, https://www.usatoday.com/story/life/allthemoms/news/2017/09/28/baltimore-library-apologizes-mug-shot-black-kids-banned-books-week/34916755/.
7. Meredith Curtis Goode, "ACLU Sues Governor Hogan for Facebook Censorship," ACLU Maryland, August 1, 2017, https://www.aclu-md.org/en/press-releases/aclu-sues-governor-hogan-facebook-censorship; "ACLU of Maine Sues LePage over Facebook Censorship," ACLU Maine, August 8, 2017, https://www.aclumaine.org/en/press-releases/aclu-maine-sues-lepage-over-facebook-censorship; "ACLU-KY Lawsuit Challenges Governor Bevin's Social Media Censorship," ACLU Kentucky, July 31, 2017, https://www.aclu.org/news/aclu-ky-lawsuit-challenges-governor-bevins-social-media-censorship.
8. Amendment by Blocking People from Social Media," *News Tribune*, July 28, 2018, https://www.thenewstribune.com/latest-news/article215468440.html.
9. Scott Bomboy, "Can Politicians Block Negative Comments on Their Social Media Accounts?" *National Constitution Center* (blog), April 5, 2018, https://constitutioncenter.org/blog/can-politicians-block-negative-comments-on-their-social-media-accounts.

10. Nivashni Nair, "School's Haunted House Gives Facebook the Horrors," Times Live, September 5, 2018, https://www.timeslive.co.za/news/south-africa/2018-09-05-schools-haunted-house-gives-facebook-the-horrors.
11. David McCabe, "Bill Clinton's Telecom Law: Twenty Years Later," The Hill, February 7, 2016, https://thehill.com/policy/technology/268459-bill-clintons-telecom-law-twenty-years-later.
12. Steve Rendall, "The Fairness Doctrine," Fair, January 1, 2005, https://fair.org/extra/the-fairness-doctrine.
13. Social Media Law Bulletin, "Glossary of U.S. Laws," https://www.socialmedialawbulletin.com/glossary-of-us-laws/.
14. ACLU, "ACLU Warns Elected Officials, Government Agencies, against Blocking Members of Public on Social Media," March 1, 2018, https://www.aclu.org/news/aclu-warns-elected-officials-government-agencies-against-blocking-members-public-social-media.
15. Oyez, "*Packingham v. North Carolina,*" Body Politic: The Supreme Court and Abortion Law, June 19, 2017, https://www.oyez.org/cases/2016/15-1194.
16. Global Freedom of Expression, "*Davison v. Loudoun County Board of Supervisors,*" Columbia University, https://globalfreedomofexpression.columbia.edu/cases/davison-v-loudoun-country-board-supervisors.
17. Leora Smith and Derek Kravitz, "Governors and Federal Agencies Are Blocking Nearly 1,300 Accounts on Facebook and Twitter," ProPublica, December 8, 2017, https://www.propublica.org/article/governors-and-federal-agencies-are-blocking-accounts-on-facebook-and-twitter.
18. Taylor & Francis Group, "Use of Social Media by the Library," https://librarianresources.taylorandfrancis.com/wp-content/uploads/2017/12/White-Paper-Social-Media-in-the-Library.pdf.
19. Cary Memorial Library, "Social Media Policy," https://www.carylibrary.org/social-media-policy.
20. Pima County, "Pima County Social Media Administrative Procedures," http://webcms.pima.gov/UserFiles/Servers/Server_6/File/Government/Administration/Administrative%20Procedures/3-31_Social_Media_Policy.pdf.
21. Kansas City Public Library, "Social Media Guidelines for Kansas City Public Library Employees," PDF.
22. Library Marketing and Communications Conference, www.librarymarketingconference.org.
23. American Library Association, "Social Media Guidelines for Public and Academic Libraries," www.ala.org/advocacy/intfreedom/socialmediaguidelines.
24. Oyez, "*Packingham v. North Carolina,*" https://www.oyez.org/cases/2016/15-1194.

6

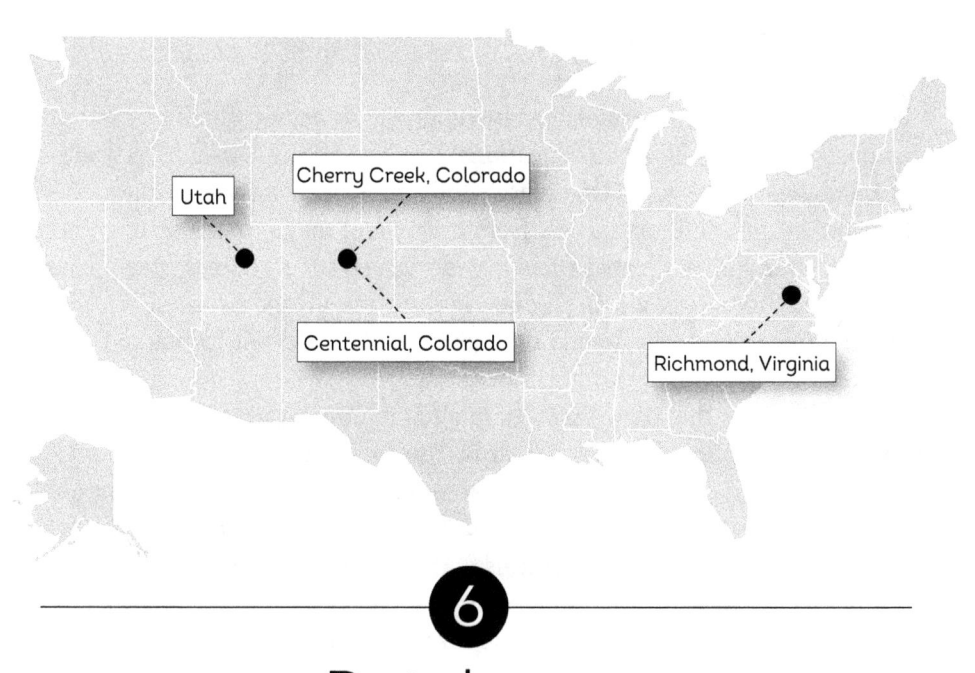

Databases

ZORA NEALE HURSTON WROTE: "RESEARCH IS FORMALIZED CURI-osity. It is poking and prying with a purpose." Though well-known for her novels and short stories, Hurston is relatively unrecognized for the anthropological and ethnographic research she conducted. During her university studies from 1918 to 1928, research for this young black woman was a struggle to attain access and equality. But Hurston's intellectual curiosity would not be squelched.

Digital Resources

To the public, databases are often a murky concept. Even many librarians would have a difficult time if they were required to fully explain what they are without using library jargon. Databases are primarily used for research. They are accessed online but they are not websites. They are a vehicle to a resource that can often be found online but also can digitalize or archive a physical resource. They are part of a collection but the collection itself is not the resource. When librarians describe databases, they often validate their use as research or scholarship but there are a lot of databases with subject content that is trade based like auto repair or popular magazines like *Time* or

People. All the content is published by reputable sources, curated by external corporations, and offered to educational institutions through subscriptions.

Databases are a popular research tool for students because they offer keyword search, full text, access from home, and they provide style guide–specific citations. A database has a wide variety of resources that are all distributed from one starting point. Library research databases get their information from professionals or experts in the field and contained published works that are already fact-checked.

The databases that libraries subscribe to are often accessed online, either on-site or from home with library cards. The database as we know it today is completely digital, but libraries used to offer similar resources in print and then on CD-ROM. The *Readers' Guide to Periodical Literature*, for example, is a reference guide to general periodicals that has been published annually since 1901, and is now available as an electronic database. Today there are hundreds of research databases available for use through library subscriptions. And within those hundreds of databases are collection subsets with specific subjects or target audiences. The leading provider of research databases, EBSCO, manages 375 full-text databases, including MEDLINE, Academic Search, NoveList, and Art Abstracts.[1]

Regardless of whether library users access a journal article online with a database, digitally or via a print index, the content is still the same. Databases just make the access to these resources easier. Which is exactly what libraries aim to do.

Problematic Periodicals

In June 2017, the ALA's Office for Intellectual Freedom started monitoring complaints about educational databases in school districts and public libraries. Organized groups of parents were broadly making accusations that many databases offered access to pornography. They were accusing EBSCO, Gale-Cengage, and other vendors of harming minors through negligence and sometimes even deliberately distributing images of sexual violence, ads for prostitution, and obscene content.

The Dirty Dozen

In 2017 an anti-pornography organization, the National Center on Sexual Exploitation (NCOSE; formerly known as "Morality in Media"), criticized

EBSCO because its databases, which are widely used in schools in the United States, "could be used to search for information about sexual terms."[2] The NCOSE placed EBSCO on its "Dirty Dozen List"—a list of organizations it describes as "major contributors to sexual exploitation," and which, this year, also included the American Library Association and the online-retailer Amazon.com. The group said that some articles from *Men's Health* and other publications indexed by EBSCO included articles with sexual (but not pornographic) content and asserted that other articles in the database linked to websites that included pornography. EBSCO responded by saying that it took the complaint seriously, but was unaware of any case "of students using its databases to access pornography or other explicit materials" and that "the searches NCOSE was concerned about had been conducted by adults actively searching for graphic materials, often on home computers that don't have the kinds of controls and filters common on school computers."

CHERRY CREEK, COLORADO

The first reports of parents searching for pornography through the EBSCO databases provided by their children's school library started surfacing in February 2017. A couple with children in the Cherry Creek School District (CO) repeatedly attended school board meetings and complained that the school's connection with the esteemed information service was leading middle-school children into a world of erotic fiction and sex toy retailers.

In 2017, the parents formed Concerned Citizens for School Databases "to increase awareness around the country that digital, school portals have been usurped to advertise and promote the $95 billion dollar sex industry."[3] On their website, they claim that "other K-12 database providers such as Cengage (GALE), ProQuest, and Overdrive have also been found to stream obscene material at minors, including live links to Zaragosa Escort Services, inviting girls to sign up." Due to persistent pressure by this small group of parents, the Cherry Creek School District ended its contract with EBSCO in September 2018.[4] Since the Cherry Creek controversy, 130 school districts nationwide have succumbed to intimidation and reportedly canceled their subscriptions with EBSCO.

UTAH EDUCATION NETWORK

In September 2018, a parent claimed to have found inappropriate materials on EBSCO's K – 12 databases and complained to the Utah Education Network

(UEN). The UEN connects all Utah school districts, schools, and higher education institutions to provide quality educational resources. After the complaint, the statewide network's board quickly voted to remove every public school district's access to EBSCO—an educational resource available to more than 700,000 students.[5] With strategic assistance from multiple organizations, the Utah Library Association and the Utah Educational Library Media Association garnered thousands of e-mails and signatures protesting the ban and urging the UEN board to restore access to EBSCO. At the board meeting and in the press, opponents of EBSCO suggested that if the board reinstated access, it would be "intentionally and knowingly" distributing pornography to minors. Almost a month later, after public feedback, collaboration with EBSCO staff, and statements by multiple educational organizations, the board voted unanimously to restore the school districts' access to the K–12 databases.

RICHMOND, VIRGINIA
During the summer of 2018, a mother of a freshman at Smithfield High School in Virginia claimed to have found adult content when searching one of Gale-Cengage's databases, which had been provided through the State Library of Virginia.[6] She contacted all the school districts in the state and then contacted the press to pressure the districts to remove the database from school resources. Many school systems use the database link on their websites. A spokeswoman for the Chesapeake Public Schools told the press: "Once alerted to the issue, CPS immediately blocked its access for use and began taking steps to remove links to this resource from all school websites."

In a public statement from Gale-Cengage, Kayla Siefker, the senior media and public relations manager, said: "It is not our role to censor content which can help young researchers gain knowledge about the issues affecting them personally—academically, medically, socially or otherwise. Rather, we work to ensure that the content they discover within our resources is accurate and comprehensive."[7]

CENTENNIAL, COLORADO
After more than 130 school districts had eliminated access to EBSCO and years of allegations, the Thomas More Society, a national nonprofit law firm "dedicated to restoring respect in law for life, family, and religious liberty," filed a lawsuit against EBSCO and the Colorado Library Consortium (CLiC).[8]

"Pornography is not education," a parent group led by the Cedar Creek School District parents said in the lawsuit, adding that EBSCO's databases contain erotic and BDSM stories that show up in non-related searches carried out by students and their parents.

Six months earlier, the CLiC executive director, Jim Duncan, had responded to the allegations and provided a guide for schools and libraries to understand and manage the attacks:[9]

> Schools and libraries possess the expertise and responsibility to choose, license/buy and manage digital content useful to their local communities. Some individuals in Colorado are attacking libraries and librarians for doing that work and are claiming that databases and e-book collections are full of pornography. These individuals are demanding a statewide ban of all databases and certain e-book products.

Duncan's guide offers practical information, strategies, and facts for libraries and schools to use in discussing this topic with their local communities, including sample challenge and reconsideration policies, solid talking points and facts, and guidance for addressing complaints and questions about filtering, plus relevant links to find more information.

The Right to Reference

Passed in 2000, the Children's Internet Protection Act (CIPA) was designed to block online images deemed "obscene," "child pornography," or "harmful to minors" by requiring public libraries and schools to install filters in order to receive federal discounts for technology. For these institutions, CIPA requires the adoption of an internet safety policy that authorizes filtering software to block images. CIPA applies only to the schools and libraries that choose to accept e-rate discounts or Library Services and Technology Act grants for their internet access. Neither obscenity nor child pornography are protected by the First Amendment. But the third criterion, "harmful to minors," pertains to sexually explicit images that are constitutionally protected for viewing by adults but lack artistic, literary, political, or scientific value for minors aged seventeen and under.[10]

The content hosted by EBSCO has all been published originally by other sources: mainstream publications, scholarly journals, statistical data, government documents, and newspapers, to name a few.[11] This content is not obscene. *Obscenity* is a legal term. Just because a person describes something as obscene, doesn't mean that it is. Only a court of law can determine if a material is obscene. Currently, obscenity is evaluated by federal and state courts alike using the Miller standard established by a 1973 Supreme Court case, *Miller v. California*. The Miller test for obscenity includes the following criteria:

1. whether "the average person, applying contemporary community standards," would find that the work, "taken as a whole," appeals to "prurient interest"
2. whether the work depicts or describes, in a patently offensive way, sexual conduct specifically defined by the applicable state law, and
3. whether the work, "taken as a whole," lacks serious literary, artistic, political, or scientific value.[12]

No obscenity charges have ever been brought against EBSCO, nor are they likely to be.

Libraries are defenders of the First Amendment. EBSCO and other databases have a right to aggregate mainstream and educational content and sell it to libraries, schools, and state agencies and consortiums. Adults have a right to read magazines, without being limited to magazines that are intended for children. Minors have a right to access information in the general marketplace.

Saving Subscribers

There has been a dramatic increase in attacks and complaints posted on social media pages about databases recently. Organized individuals and groups are systematically and virtually visiting public library and school districts and are leaving one-star reviews for those districts and libraries that they accuse of supporting pornography for minors by subscribing to a database vendor.

If the challenge to a database subscription comes over the internet, on Facebook, through e-mail, or from someone who does not reside in the district or community, the professional obligation may extend no farther than a polite thank-you. But if the person who comments via social media is a local user, directing them to an appropriate channel for their comment would be best practice. Databases are library resources just like books, and to consider removing access to them or canceling subscriptions to them should go through the appropriate reconsideration policy. In general, libraries should refrain from discussing the merits of their resources on social media channels. Most reconsideration policies involve a face-to-face meeting where a patron or parent can express his or her concerns and ask questions about what is accessible via the database and what precautions are in place.

Libraries and schools should take the time needed for staff and administrators to familiarize themselves with the specific products included in their license and speak to EBSCO representatives about what options are available, should they want to make alterations to the content they provide. In its 2017 statement, EBSCO said:

> EBSCO databases are often purchased at the state level and are provided to a wide range of institutions that serve many age groups. The intent is for each institution to provide access to the appropriate databases. While EBSCO provides guidance as to which databases are appropriate for K-12 use, it is possible that a given school or district may expose the full suite of resources, unintentionally providing access to resources that may not be considered completely age-appropriate. In these cases, we are working with customers to switch to age-appropriate versions of databases as recommended.[13]

Public libraries don't restrict all of their content, digital or physical, to what is suitable for children. They serve all of the public. Most libraries specifically do not limit access to materials by age. The purpose of this policy, however, is not to push adult content on people too young for it. Rather, people tend to naturally gravitate to information that is appropriate to their age. Libraries have children's rooms, but they also allow children to check out books from the whole collection when they demonstrate interest in those resources. Even in school libraries that serve a broad range of students, from kindergarten to the twelfth grade, librarians don't restrict content for all based on the youngest users.

In all of these attacks on databases, whether on social media, e-mail, or in the press, the language is inflammatory and provocative. The groups targeting libraries and schools want to shame and scare administrators into immediate action. James LaRue points out in an article for the *Journal of*

Intellectual Freedom and Privacy that the "ALA's Office for Intellectual Freedom is aware of no reports of any minor seeking or finding illegal or even pornographic content through EBSCO."[14] In every report, the searches are completed by adults, usually parents, with far more skill and a definite motivation. These searches are also conducted at home, and off school premises, where the internet connection is less likely to be filtered.

Reconsideration Policies

Parents, patrons, community groups, and national organizations like NCOSE are free to protest sexual images and articles, and to advocate for their elimination in publications. But they are limited in restricting access to themselves and their families. Libraries do have a responsibility to listen to the concerns of their constituents, however. The best practice for providing a procedure to hear those concerns is to adopt a "Request for Reconsideration" policy. When a patron expresses concern about content, a thoughtful process calls for dialogue between those involved, and possibly a committee to examine the challenged resource or service. In 2018, the ALA's "Selection and Reconsideration Policy Toolkit for Public, School and Academic Libraries" was updated to facilitate libraries in protecting resources and the intellectual freedom of their users.[15] The policy toolkit covers not just books, but also digital resources like databases. It's not uncommon for libraries and school districts to overlook their well-established policies when complaints are submitted about databases because of the misconceived notion that censorship only affects books.

Selection and reconsideration policies are designed to broadly cover all library resources, from books to films, music, magazines, and yes, even databases. Policies outline how libraries select which databases to use, what the purpose of the purchase is, and how it will benefit the overall mission of the organization. The policies consider the framework of libraries and their role within the larger community. The policies provide a means to an objective and thoughtful consideration of resources in an efficient manner. Many reconsideration processes also allow an appeal to the governing body of the library. The decision of that authority is considered final.

The following are some questions for a library to consider when updating selection and reconsideration policies in order to protect its databases:

- Has the library completed a thorough audit of all digital resources, including databases and streaming content?
- Are there different criteria for youth resources vs. adult resources?
- Are youth restricted from accessing adult database collections?
- Is it clear how to submit a complaint or concern about digital resources?
- Are search results filtered? If so, how are the filters implemented?
- Are librarians empowered to unblock resources if requested?
- Is the level of control that administrators have clear to staff and trustees?
- Is it clear to staff and trustees what, if any, customizations have been activated by the database vendors?
- Is off-site access to databases the same as on-site access?

Relevant Interpretations of the *Library Bill of Rights*

Libraries are major sources of information for society, and they serve as guardians of the public's access to information. The advent of the digital world has revolutionized how the public obtains its information and how libraries provide it. As the digital world continues to evolve, libraries help ensure that people can access the information they need—regardless of their age, education, ethnicity, language, income, physical limitations, or geographic barriers. The core values of the library community—such as equal access to information, intellectual freedom, and the objective stewardship and provision of information—must be preserved and strengthened, now more than ever.

The 2009 *Library Bill of Rights* interpretation "Access to Digital Information, Services, and Networks" explicitly states: "Libraries empower users by offering opportunities both for accessing the broadest range of information created by others and for creating and sharing information. Digital resources enhance the ability of libraries to fulfill this responsibility."[16] In 2015, the ALA Council adopted an interpretation of the *Library Bill of Rights* on "Internet Filtering." (See "Access to Digital Information, Services, and Networks;" "Internet Filtering," and other interpretations of the *Library Bill of Rights* in the Appendix.)

> CIPA-mandated content filtering has had three significant impacts in our schools and libraries. First, it has widened the divide between those

who can afford to pay for personal access and those who must depend on publicly funded (and filtered) access. Second, when content filtering is deployed to limit access to what some may consider objectionable or offensive, often minority viewpoints religions, or controversial topics are included in the categories of what is considered objectionable or offensive. Filters thus become the tool of bias and discrimination and marginalize users by denying or abridging their access to these materials. Finally, when over-blocking occurs in public libraries and schools, library users, educators, and students who lack other means of access to the Internet are limited to the content allowed by unpredictable and unreliable filters.[17]

EBSCO, Gale-Cengage, Overdrive, and other databases are longtime, well-respected distributors of educational content that is used nationally in libraries and schools, across grade levels and subject areas and accessible to all students, both rural and urban. The ability to search, evaluate, and select information is integral to student success in the classroom, in post-secondary education, and in the workplace. The imperative of teachers and librarians to cultivate this skill in our youth is vital to an informed citizenry for the next generation.

To Be Continued

The challenges directed against databases are in fact an organized and ongoing attack against education. Many of the parents who initially complained or spoke directly to the press in these cases are connected with the National Center on Sexual Exploitation and with Family Watch International. These organizations, marked as anti-LGBTQ extremist groups by the Southern Poverty Law Center,[18] try to ban EBSCO from schools and libraries. When blogging about "the international database scandal" for *Meridian Magazine*, a parent said: "Schools and libraries have been categorized by the United States as 'safe places' for children. Sadly, the majority of these 'safe places' are exploiting children by spoon feeding them pornographic images, videos, and illicit sexual articles through databases."[19] She also implored her readers to not only look at school library databases, but also investigate public libraries and colleges because it is "a lie that the databases are safe." The tone and content of this blog make it clear that there is a larger targeted attack on schools, public libraries, and colleges.

NOTES

1. EBSCO, "Frequently Asked Questions," https://help.ebsco.com/interfaces/EBSCOhost/EBSCOhost_FAQs.

2. Jackie Zubrzycki, "Do Online Databases Filter Out Enough Inappropriate Material?" *Education Week* (blog), July 14, 2017, http://blogs.edweek.org/edweek/curriculum/2017/07/EBSCO_online_databases_filter_inappropriate_material.html.

3. "An Open Response to the Colorado Library Consortium (CLiC) Regarding Pornography in the EBSCO Databases Made Available to the Children by Schools and Libraries," *Concerned Citizens for School Databases* (blog), April 30, 2018, http://ccsdconversations.org/2018/04/30/an-open-response-to-the-colorado-library-consortium-clic-regarding-pornography-in-the-ebsco-databases-made-available-to-children-by-schools-and-libraries.

4. Grant Stringer, "Cherry Creek Schools Ditches EBSCO Student Database after Prolonged Complaints about Accessible Porn," *The Sentinel*, September 4, 2018, https://www.sentinelcolorado.com/news/metro/education/cherry-creek-schools-ditches-ebsco-student-database-after-prolonged-complaints-about-accessible-pornography/.

5. Marjorie Cortez, "Divided State School Board Supports Restoring Student, Educator Access to Blocked Database," *Deseret News*, October 4, 2018, https://www.deseretnews.com/article/900035156/divided-state-school-board-supports-restoring-student-educator-access-to-blocked-database.html.

6. Chris Horne, "Mother's Complaint about 'Very Explicit' Links Prompts IOW Schools to Change Website," WAVY.com, September 4, 2018, https://www.wavy.com/news/local-news/isle-of-wight/mother-s-complaint-about-very-explicit-links-prompts-iow-schools-to-change-website/1417440607.

7. Kayla Siefker, "Statement from Gale-Cengage," statement to WAVY.com, https://media.wavy.com/nxs-wavytv-media-us-east-1/document_dev/2018/09/05/SMITHFIELD%20CONTENT_1536158136888_54284365_ver1.0.pdf.

8. "Pornography Hidden in School Children's Databases: Parents Sue Educational Tech Company," Thomas More Society, October 10, 2018, https://www.thomasmoresociety.org/pornography-hidden-in-school-childrens-databases-parents-sue-educational-tech-company/; Monte Whaley, "Parent Group Sues Colorado Library Consortium over Database It Alleges Gives Kids Access to Pornography," Denver Post, October 10, 2018, https://www.denverpost.com/2018/10/10/pornography-is-not-education-sues-colorado-library-consortium.

9. Jim Duncan, "Libraries under Attack," Colorado Library Consortium, March 21, 2018, https://www.clicweb.org/libraries-under-attack.

10. Children's Internet Protection Act of 2000, 47 U.S.C. 254.
11. EBSCO, "The Most Comprehensive Collection of Content," https://www.ebscohost.com/discovery/content.
12. Cornell Law School, "Obscenity," https://www.law.cornell.edu/wex/obscenity.
13. James LaRue, "False Witness: Morality in Media and EBSCO," *Journal of Intellectual Freedom and Privacy*, fall 2017.
14. EBSCO, "EBSCO Information Services (EBSCO) Has Enhanced Its Efforts to Limit Inappropriate Content in Products for Schools while Providing Valuable Tools to Enhance Student Education," statement to WBRC (Birmingham, AL), June 28, 2017, http://wbrc.images.worldnow.com/library/df744b52-539d-4717-81b8-b443ee881c51.pdf.
15. American Library Association, "Selection and Reconsideration Policy Toolkit for Public, School, and Academic Libraries," www.ala.org/tools/challengesupport/selectionpolicytoolkit.
16. American Library Association, "Access to Digital Information, Services, and Networks," www.ala.org/advocacy/intfreedom/librarybill/interpretations/accessdigital.
17. American Library Association, "Internet Filtering," www.ala.org/advocacy/intfreedom/librarybill/interpretations/internet-filtering.
18. Southern Poverty Law Center, "Family Watch International," https://www.splcenter.org/fighting-hate/extremist-files/group/family-watch-international.
19. Nicholeen Peck, "When 'Safe Places' Are No Longer Safe for Your Children," *Meridian Magazine*, October 10, 2018, https://ldsmag.com/when-safe-places-are-no-longer-safe-for-your-children.

7

Report and Support

JAMES LARUE, FORMER DIRECTOR OF THE ALA'S OFFICE FOR INTEL-lectual Freedom (OIF), frequently writes and speaks on the need to discuss issues and occurrences of censorship. He is quoted as saying: "Censorship thrives in silence; silence is its aim."

Reporting challenges to the OIF raises our awareness of the harms of censorship. The OIF tracks attempts to remove or restrict materials and services in libraries and schools across the country. The more information that is brought to light about challenges and bans, the more education and resources the OIF can provide to librarians.

Censors and Selectors

A *challenge* is a direct request to a library, school, or university to remove or restrict materials or services due to their content or appropriateness. Often these requests are submitted via a formal, written complaint or a reconsideration form; and sometimes they are not. But any time a request or action impacts the rights of others in the community or institution to access a material or service, that request falls within the definition of a challenge. Sometimes challenges do not follow official procedure. With the rise of social media, more and more complaints are published online that express outrage at an institution, its policies, or its materials or services. When public support for a challenge has attracted enough attention—in the form of a petition, a Twitter storm, or a public protest—to warrant action by the library or governing body, the American Library Association asks for a report so the library can be supported and the incident can be documented. These situations qualify as a challenge.

A ban is the removal of materials or the canceling of services because of complaints or challenges, or due to the misuse of institutional authority. While situations occur where a reconsideration committee or governing board may vote to ban material, it is more common that materials are banned, services canceled, or resources denied because a library did not follow its policy and acted unethically and illegally.

A decision to ban is not the same as a professional selection decision not to carry material or offer a program because it doesn't align with local selection policies, which consider a variety of criteria when offering resources. Once a resource has been determined to meet selection criteria and is a part of the collection or the resources offered, to remove it violates the First Amendment rights of library users or students. It is important that librarians rely upon adopted policies and their own professional judgment and skills to determine what programs, resources, services, and displays best meet the mission of the library and the needs of its users. Any decision to restrict or deny access is most appropriately made by individual users or their families, who are best equipped to know and understand their own intellectual and emotional development. But it is not the obligation or right of others to restrict an individual's ability to read or learn from a resource.

In 1953 Lester Asheim published the article "Not Censorship but Selection," where he describes the fundamental differences between the "selector" and the "censor" in the clearest terms:[1]

> For to the selector, the important thing is to find reasons to keep the book. Given such a guiding principle, the selector looks for values, for strengths, for virtues which will overshadow minor objections. For the censor, on the other hand, the important thing is to find reasons to reject the book; his guiding principle leads him to seek out the objectionable features, the weaknesses, the possibilities for misinterpretation. The positive selector asks what the reaction of a rational intelligent adult would be to the content of the work; the censor fears for the

results on the weak, the warped, and the irrational. The selector says, if there is anything good in this book, let us try to keep it; the censor says, if there is anything bad in this book, let us reject it. And since there is seldom a flawless work in any form, the censor's approach can destroy much that is worth saving.

These fundamental distinctions have not changed with the much broader array of resources and services that libraries offer now. Whether it's a book or a program, a display, an artwork, an online database, or a tweet, a selector's motivation is to provide value for a user: information, enjoyment, or identity. When the motivation is to remove content out of fear of offending someone, it becomes the action of a censor.

If You See Something, Say Something

By reporting censorship incidents, librarians and educators help to identify trends in censorship cases and document their institutions' responses and solutions to censorship. Since 1990, the OIF has maintained a database on censorship challenges in libraries, schools, and universities. This data is collected from two sources: volunteer reports submitted by individuals, media reports, and public documents.

FIGURE 7.1
Office for Intellectual Freedom report graphic

Scope

The scope of the reports is broad, but there are limitations. The First Amendment specifically addresses public institutions that are representatives of our government. The Institute of Museum and Library Services, an independent federal agency, defines a public library as an institution that is "established under state enabling laws or regulations to serve a community, district, or region, and provides at least the following: an organized collection of printed or other library materials, or a combination thereof; paid staff; an established schedule in which services of the staff are available to the public; the facilities necessary to support such a collection, staff, and schedule, and is supported in whole or in part with public funds." There is nothing in this definition about profit, popular demand, retail, best-sellers, publishing, merchandise, sales, owners, or advertisements. Libraries are nonprofit institutions that serve everyone and provide access to all ideas—for free.

Public libraries, like public schools, public universities, public agencies, public parks, and city departments, are enacted and structured through local governments authorized by the people and are organized by municipal, state, and federal laws. Those people who work in a public library are considered civil servants and employees of the local government.

When decisions are made by a school board, library board, board of regents, provost, mayor, city council, or the teachers, librarians, faculty, and staff they employ, those decisions are made by the government. And the First Amendment to the U.S. Constitution prevents the government from "respecting an establishment of religion," prohibiting the free exercise of religion, or abridging the freedom of speech, the freedom of the press, the right to peaceably assemble, or to petition for a governmental redress of grievances. Because of this, the OIF limits its scope to public institutions in the United States.

Traditionally, censorship reports have centered on banned books: fiction, nonfiction, children's books, books for young adults, books for adults, and books for educational or recreational reading. But as the scope of libraries' services has grown, and as our awareness of censorship has intensified, there are more reports about programs, displays, databases, artwork, magazines, DVDs, music, and social media being censored. Librarians are encouraged to report anything they are concerned about, even if they are unsure if it falls within the scope of what the OIF tracks. In tracking media accounts of incidents outside its scope, the OIF may note issues that are related to independent booksellers, campus speakers, international incidents, publishing, and free speech conflicts, but rarely is there ALA involvement or an outreach of support in these cases. The OIF's main focus is on libraries and on supporting librarians when resources are challenged.

Data

The ALA tracks a lot of information in order to connect as many dots as possible and thus form a larger national picture of censorship:

- Who is censoring materials?
- Are challenge requests coming from parents, religious institutions, politicians, or organized groups?
- What are their concerns? What reasons did they express in their communication?
- Are items being pulled because of racist language, profanity, or nudity?
- What issues are relevant in the materials and services that indicate there is a larger concern, over and above the reason listed for the challenge?
- How many displays are dismantled because of complaints?
- Are the majority of challenges happening in public libraries or in academic institutions?
- Are institutions following board-approved policies when they respond to a challenge?
- What types of materials are challenged?
- How was the situation resolved?
- What is the racial makeup, religion, or sexual identity of the authors or creators of the content involved?
- Who is the intended audience for the resource?
- Is the challenge confidential or public?

This information helps the ALA prioritize its resources and strategically focus its energy in ways that will help the profession. The data is often compiled and presented in infographics and reports in order to support educational efforts about censorship.

While priority is given to protecting confidentiality and the trust of those who report censorship to the OIF, reports that are not confidential are included in internal reports for OIF members and are often published in the annual field report, or in banned book resource guides like *Banned Books: Defending Our Freedom to Read* by Robert P. Doyle. This information is helpful because students, teachers, and reporters often inquire about specific resources that have been challenged and why. As long as librarians are not requesting that the situation be kept confidential, the OIF will use the data to further the enlightenment of the library profession and the public.

Silent Censorship

There are some genuine barriers to reporting censorship. Often people don't know how to report it. Some front-line staff may think that reporting it is a supervisor's responsibility. Some librarians may fear they'll be admonished for reporting censorship. Some administrators don't want to report it out of fear of stirring controversy or bad publicity. And some library systems or school districts just don't think it's the ALA's business.

Article 3 of the ALA *Library Bill of Rights* states: "Libraries should challenge censorship in the fulfillment of their responsibility to provide information and enlightenment." Reporting censorship is a professional obligation. The more that is known, and the more data that is gathered, the more support the professional community can provide for library workers of all types. This knowledge helps prepare library administrations and communities to advocate for libraries as fundamental building blocks of democracy.

Multiple state reports have provided data that demonstrate the gross underreporting of censorship that is handicapping the profession. The OIF compared data from the University of Missouri's School of Journalism, the Oregon Intellectual Freedom Clearinghouse, and the Texas ACLU with reports submitted to the American Library Association.[2] In those studies, the organizations each compiled their own data on challenges and censorship, using Freedom of Information Act requests or their own methods for asking libraries about reporting. When the OIF studied that data and compared it

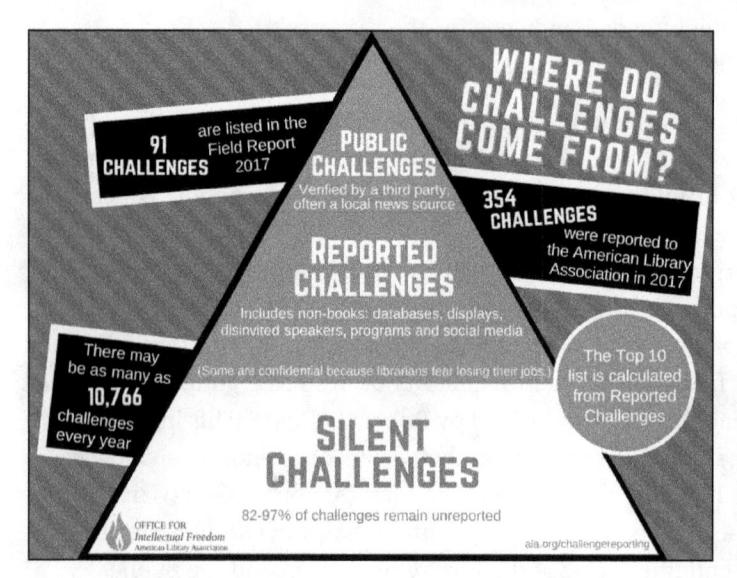

FIGURE 7.2 Infographic Triangle: Pyramid of Silent censorship

to what actually gets reported to the ALA, it found that an estimated 82–97 percent of censorship incidents go unreported to the ALA.

The Importance of Professional Support

Reporting censorship helps the OIF to provide better information and support to librarians and teachers who are facing intellectual freedom challenges. As a professional association, supporting librarians is a high priority for the ALA.

Anyone may contact the ALA with questions or to report a challenge to library or classroom resources via an online challenge reporting form. The person does not have to be a member of the ALA or a librarian. The ALA follows the lead of the people it is working with. But in some situations, publicly aligning with an external national advocate like the ALA may not be the best course of action for a librarian in a tenuous environment. Confidentiality and protecting librarians are, after all, paramount considerations. While exposing censorship and shedding light on misuses of power are the best way to protect intellectual freedom, these can't be at the sacrifice of librarians' jobs or security. There are real-life situations where librarians fear losing their jobs or experience other negative repercussions for speaking out. Working on the front lines can be challenging. If a case is reported in the media or listed in public documents, the ALA may include the institution in reports, but it would keep confidential its support and interactions with a librarian who doesn't wish to be mentioned publicly.

Professional and personal support can take many different forms and can be different for each person who contacts the OIF. About half the reports that are submitted have already been resolved, and the institution simply reports the case as a final duty of the procedure. The complaint was received by the institution, it was handled smoothly according to their policies, the situation was resolved, and the case was closed. Sometimes the report comes in to the OIF directly after the resolution, but sometimes it comes in months or even years later.

The other reports that are submitted usually are seeking answers to questions, guidance in the process, validation of their decisions, or personal encouragement and solidarity:

- Has the resource been challenged before?
- Can you help me find book reviews about this title?

- I'm looking for an article that supports displays on world religions. Where should I start?
- How do we host a challenge hearing?
- I really don't think it's appropriate to use that word in a classroom. Is it censorship if I think the parent is right?
- Are there legal cases that I can share with my board about hate speech?
- How much time should the committee members be allowed to read the material and supplemental materials?
- Our policy is outdated. Can I update it before the board meeting?
- How should I respond to these angry voicemails?
- Has anyone else ever gone through a challenge like this before?
- Can the ALA write a letter to the board supporting our recommendation to retain the book?
- Do I have to provide interviews to the press? I'm so nervous I'm going to say the wrong thing.
- What if I'm fired?

Supporting librarians and educators involves a lot of listening. A challenge situation can be one of the most stressful and loneliest times in a librarian's life. Librarians have expressed feeling attacked and abandoned by their community and their colleagues. They are doubtful about their own decisions and morals. These feelings and questions are personal and subjective, and they often occupy morally ambiguous areas. Oftentimes, two values will seem to be in contradiction with each other. The questions listed above are all tough questions, and more often than is comfortable for professionals, there is no one right answer. The best way to come to a good solution for the community and the library users who are involved in the controversy is to have the tough conversations and talk the issue out. By soliciting multiple perspectives, listening to other people, and evaluating professional principles and policies, a solid, respectable, and transparent decision can often be reached.

Free speech is not easy.

> Understand, democracy does not require uniformity. Our founders quarreled and compromised and expected us to do the same. But they knew that democracy does require a basic sense of solidarity—the idea

that for all our outward differences, we are all in this together; that we rise or fall as one.

—*Barack Obama*

NOTES

1. Lester Asheim, "Not Censorship but Selection," *Wilson Library Bulletin* 28 (September 1953): 63–67.
2. University of Missouri School of Journalism, "Journalism Students Produce 10-Part Series on Book Challenges in Missouri's Public Schools: The 'Unfit to Read' Project Provides Hands-on Experience with Sunshine Requests," https://journalism.missouri.edu/2012/07/journalism-students-produce-10-part-series-on-book-challenges-in-missouris-public-schools; Concordia University Libraries, "Banned Books Week: Frequently Challenged: U.S. & Oregon," http://libguides.cu-portland.edu/banned_books/challenged; American Civil Liberties Union of Texas, "Free People Read Freely: 15th Annual Report on Challenged and Banned Books in Texas Public Schools" (PDF), https://www.aclutx.org/sites/default/files/field_documents/bb2k11.pdf.

APPENDIX

The Library Bill of Rights

The American Library Association affirms that all libraries are forums for information and ideas, and that the following basic policies should guide their services.

I. Books and other library resources should be provided for the interest, information, and enlightenment of all people of the community the library serves. Materials should not be excluded because of the origin, background, or views of those contributing to their creation.

II. Libraries should provide materials and information presenting all points of view on current and historical issues. Materials should not be proscribed or removed because of partisan or doctrinal disapproval.

III. Libraries should challenge censorship in the fulfillment of their responsibility to provide information and enlightenment.

IV. Libraries should cooperate with all persons and groups concerned with resisting abridgment of free expression and free access to ideas.

V. A person's right to use a library should not be denied or abridged because of origin, age, background, or views.

VI. Libraries which make exhibit spaces and meeting rooms available to the public they serve should make such facilities available on an equitable basis, regardless of the beliefs or affiliations of individuals or groups requesting their use.

VII. All people, regardless of origin, age, background, or views, possess a right to privacy and confidentiality in their library use. Libraries should advocate for, educate about, and protect people's privacy, safeguarding all library use data, including personally identifiable information.

Adopted June 19, 1939, by the ALA Council; amended October 14, 1944; June 18, 1948; February 2, 1961; June 27, 1967; January 23, 1980; inclusion of "age" reaffirmed January 23, 1996.

APPENDIX

Access to Digital Information, Services, and Networks

An Interpretation of the Library Bill of Rights

Introduction

Freedom of expression is an inalienable human right and the foundation for self-government. Freedom of expression encompasses the freedom of speech and the corollary right to receive information.[1] Libraries and librarians protect and promote these rights regardless of the format or technology employed to create and disseminate information.

The American Library Association expresses the fundamental principles of librarianship in its *Code of Ethics* as well as in the *Library Bill of Rights* and its Interpretations. These principles guide librarians and library governing bodies in addressing issues of intellectual freedom that arise when the library provides access to digital information, services, and networks.

Libraries empower users by offering opportunities both for accessing the broadest range of information created by others and for creating and sharing information. Digital resources enhance the ability of libraries to fulfill this responsibility.

Libraries should regularly review issues arising from digital creation, distribution, retrieval, and archiving of information in the context of constitutional principles and ALA policies so that fundamental and traditional tenets of librarianship are upheld. Although digital information flows across boundaries and barriers despite attempts by individuals, governments, and private entities to channel or control it, many people lack access or capability to use or create digital information effectively.

101

In making decisions about how to offer access to digital information, services, and networks, each library should consider intellectual freedom principles in the context of its mission, goals, objectives, cooperative agreements, and the needs of the entire community it serves.

The Rights of Users

All library system and network policies, procedures, or regulations relating to digital information and services should be scrutinized for potential violation of user rights. User policies should be developed according to the policies and guidelines established by the American Library Association, including "Guidelines for the Development and Implementation of Policies, Regulations, and Procedures Affecting Access to Library Materials, Services, and Facilities."

Users' access should not be restricted or denied for expressing, receiving, creating, or participating in constitutionally protected speech. If access is restricted or denied for behavioral or other reasons, users should be provided due process, including, but not limited to, formal notice and a means of appeal.

Information retrieved, utilized, or created digitally is constitutionally protected unless determined otherwise by a court of competent jurisdiction. These rights extend to minors as well as adults ("Access to Library Resources and Services for Minors"; "Access to Resources and Services in the School Library"; and "Minors and Internet Activity").[2]

Libraries should use technology to enhance, not deny, digital access. Users have the right to be free of unreasonable limitations or conditions set by libraries, librarians, system administrators, vendors, network service providers, or others. Contracts, agreements, and licenses entered into by libraries on behalf of their users should not violate this right. Libraries should provide library users the training and assistance necessary to find, evaluate, and use information effectively.

Users have both the right of confidentiality and the right of privacy. The library should uphold these rights by policy, procedure, and practice in accordance with "Privacy: An Interpretation of the *Library Bill of Rights*," and "Advocating for Intellectual Freedom: An Interpretation of the *Library Bill of Rights*."

Equity of Access

The digital environment provides expanding opportunities for everyone to participate in the information society, but individuals may face serious barriers to access.

Digital information, services, and networks provided directly or indirectly by the library should be equally, readily, and equitably accessible to all library users. American Library Association policies oppose the charging of user fees for the provision of information services by libraries that receive support from public funds.[3] All libraries should develop policies concerning access to digital information that are consistent with ALA's policies and guidelines, including "Economic Barriers to Information Access: An Interpretation of the *Library Bill of Rights*," "Guidelines for the Development and Implementation of Policies, Regulations and Procedures Affecting Access to Library Materials, Services and Facilities," and "Services to Persons with Disabilities: An Interpretation of the *Library Bill of Rights*."

Information Resources and Access

Libraries, acting within their mission and objectives, must support access to information on all subjects that serve the needs or interests of each user, regardless of the user's age or the content of the material. In order to preserve the cultural record and to prevent the loss of information, libraries may need to expand their selection or collection development policies to ensure preservation, in appropriate formats, of information obtained digitally. Libraries have an obligation to provide access to government information available in digital format.

Providing connections to global information, services, and networks is not the same as selecting and purchasing materials for a library collection. Libraries and librarians should not deny or limit access to digital information because of its allegedly controversial content or because of a librarian's personal beliefs or fear of confrontation. Furthermore, libraries and librarians should not deny access to digital information solely on the grounds that it is perceived to lack value. Parents and legal guardians who are concerned about their children's use of digital resources should provide guidance to their own children. Some information accessed digitally may not meet a library's selection or collection development policy. It is, therefore, left to each user to determine what is appropriate.

Publicly funded libraries have a legal obligation to provide access to constitutionally protected information. Federal, state, county, municipal, local, or library governing bodies sometimes require the use of internet filters or other technological measures that block access to constitutionally protected information, contrary to the *Library Bill of Rights*.[4] If a library uses a technological measure that blocks access to information, it should be set at the least restrictive level in order to minimize the blocking of constitutionally protected speech. Adults retain the right to access all constitutionally protected information and to ask for the technological measure to be disabled in a timely manner. Minors also retain the right to access constitutionally protected information and, at the minimum, have the right to ask the library or librarian to provide access to erroneously blocked information in a timely manner. Libraries and librarians have an obligation to inform users of these rights and to provide the means to exercise these rights.[5]

Digital resources provide unprecedented opportunities to expand the scope of information available to users. Libraries and librarians should provide access to information presenting all points of view. The provision of access does not imply sponsorship or endorsement. These principles pertain to digital resources as much as they do to the more traditional sources of information in libraries ("Diversity in Collection Development").

NOTES

1. *Martin v. Struthers*, 319 U.S. 141 (1943); *Lamont v. Postmaster General*, 381 U.S. 301 (1965); Susan Nevelow Mart, "The Right to Receive Information," 95 *Law Library Journal* 2 (2003).

2. Tinker v. Des Moines Independent Community School District, 393 U.S. 503 (1969); Board of Education, Island Trees Union Free School District No. 26 v. Pico, 457 U.S. 853 (1982); American Amusement Machine Association v. Teri Kendrick, 244 F.3d 954 (7th Cir. 2001); cert.denied, 534 U.S. 994 (2001).

3. ALA Policy Manual, 50.3 "Free Access to Information"; 53.1.14 "Economic Barriers to Information Access"; 60.1.1 "Minority Concerns Policy Objectives"; 61.1 "Library Services for the Poor: Policy Objectives."

4. ALA Policy Manual, 53.1.17, "Resolution on the Use of Filtering Software in Libraries."

5. "If some libraries do not have the capacity to unblock specific Web sites or to disable the filter or if it is shown that an adult user's election to view

constitutionally protected Internet material is burdened in some other substantial way, that would be the subject for an as-applied challenge, not the facial challenge made in this case." *United States, et al. v. American Library Association*, 539 U.S. 194 (2003) (Justice Kennedy, concurring).

Adopted January 24, 1996; amended January 19, 2005; and July 15, 2009, by the ALA Council.

References to cited policies have been updated on November 6, 2018.

APPENDIX

Access to Library Resources and Services Regardless of Sex, Gender Identity, Gender Expression, or Sexual Orientation

An Interpretation of the Library Bill of Rights

American libraries exist and function within the context of a body of laws derived from the United States Constitution and the First Amendment. The *Library Bill of Rights* embodies the basic policies that guide libraries in the provision of services, materials, and programs.

In the preamble to its *Library Bill of Rights*, the American Library Association affirms that all libraries are forums for information and ideas. This concept of forum and its accompanying principle of inclusiveness pervade all six Articles of the *Library Bill of Rights*.

The American Library Association stringently and unequivocally maintains that libraries and librarians have an obligation to resist efforts that systematically exclude materials dealing with any subject matter, including sex, gender identity, gender expression, or sexual orientation:

Article I of the *Library Bill of Rights* states that "Materials should not be excluded because of the origin, background, or views of those contributing to their creation. "The Association affirms that books and other materials coming from presses that specialize in gay, lesbian, bisexual, and/or transgender subject matter; gay, lesbian, bisexual and/or transgender authors or other creators; and materials regardless of format or services dealing with gay, lesbian, bisexual and/or transgender life are protected by the *Library Bill of Rights*. Librarians are obligated by the *Library Bill of Rights* to endeavor to select materials without regard to the sex, gender identity, or sexual orientation of their creators by using the criteria identified in their written, approved selection policies.[1]

Article II maintains that "Libraries should provide materials and information presenting all points of view on current and historical issues. Materials should not be proscribed or removed because of partisan or doctrinal disapproval." Library services, materials, and programs representing diverse points of view on sex, gender identity, gender expression, or sexual orientation should be considered for purchase and inclusion in library collections and programs.[2,3,4] The Association affirms that attempts to proscribe or remove materials dealing with gay, lesbian, bisexual, and/or transgender life without regard to the written, approved selection policy violate this tenet and constitute censorship.

Articles III and IV mandate that libraries "challenge censorship" and cooperate with those "resisting abridgement of free expression and free access to ideas."

Article V holds that "A person's right to use a library should not be denied or abridged because of origin, age, background or views." In the *Library Bill of Rights* and all its Interpretations, it is intended that: "origin" encompasses all the characteristics of individuals that are inherent in the circumstances of their birth; "age" encompasses all the characteristics of individuals that are inherent in their levels of development and maturity; "background" encompasses all the characteristics of individuals that are a result of their life experiences; and "views" encompasses all the opinions and beliefs held and expressed by individuals. Therefore, Article V of the *Library Bill of Rights* mandates that library services, materials, and programs be available to all members of the community the library serves, without regard to sex, gender identity, gender expression, or sexual orientation. This includes providing youth with comprehensive sex education literature.

Article VI maintains that "Libraries which make exhibit spaces and meeting rooms available to the public they serve should make such facilities available on an equitable basis, regardless of the beliefs or affiliations of individuals or groups requesting their use." This protection extends to all groups and members of the community the library serves, without regard to sex, gender identity, gender expression, or sexual orientation.

The American Library Association holds that any attempt, be it legal or extra-legal, to regulate or suppress library services, materials, or programs must be resisted in order that protected expression is not abridged. Librarians have a professional obligation to ensure that all library users have free and equal access to the entire range of library services, materials, and programs. Therefore, the Association strongly opposes any effort to limit access to information and ideas. The Association also encourages librarians to proactively support the First Amendment rights of all library users, regardless of sex, gender identity, gender expression, or sexual orientation.

NOTES

1. "Evaluating Library Collections: An Interpretation of the *Library Bill of Rights*," adopted February 2, 1973, by the ALA Council; amended July 1, 1981; June 2, 2008.
2. "Challenged Resources: An Interpretation of the *Library Bill of Rights*," adopted June 25, 1971 by the ALA Council; amended July 1, 1981; January 10, 1990; January 28, 2009; and July 1, 2014.
3. "Meeting Rooms: An Interpretation of the *Library Bill of Rights*," adopted July 2, 1991, by the ALA Council; amended June 26, 2018.
4. "Diversity in Collection Development: An Interpretation of the *Library Bill of Rights*," adopted July 14, 1982, by the ALA Council; amended January 10, 1990; July 2, 2008; and July 1, 2014.

Adopted June 30, 1993, by the ALA Council; amended July 12, 2000, June 30, 2004; and July 2, 2008.

APPENDIX

Challenged Resources

An Interpretation of the Library Bill of Rights

Libraries: An American Value" states, "We protect the rights of individuals to express their opinions about library resources and services."[1] The American Library Association declares as a matter of firm principle that it is the responsibility of every library to have a clearly defined written policy for collection development that includes a procedure for review of challenged resources. Collection development applies to library materials and resources in all formats, programs, and services.

Article I of the American Library Association's Library Bill of Rights states, "Materials should not be excluded because of the origin, background, or views of those contributing to their creation." Article II further declares, "Materials should not be proscribed or removed because of partisan or doctrinal disapproval."

Freedom of expression, although it can be offensive to some, is protected by the Constitution of the United States. The "Diversity in Collection Development: An Interpretation of the Library Bill of Rights" states:

Librarians have a professional responsibility to be fair, just, and equitable and to give all library users equal protection in guarding against violation of the library patron's right to read, view, or listen to content protected by the First Amendment, no matter what the viewpoint of the author, creator, or selector. Librarians have an obligation to protect library collections from removal of content based on personal bias or prejudice.[2]

This applies with equal force to library resources and services provided to students and minors.[3]

The Supreme Court has held that the Constitution requires a procedure designed to critically examine all challenged expression before it can be suppressed.[4] Therefore, libraries should develop a procedure by which the governing body examines concerns and challenges about library resources. This procedure should be open, transparent, and conform to all applicable open meeting and public records laws. Challenged resources should remain in the collection, and access to the resources remain unrestricted during the review process. Resources that meet the criteria for selection and inclusion within the collection as outlined in the institution's collections policy should not be removed. Procedures to review challenges to library resources should not be used to suppress constitutionally protected expression.

Any attempt, be it legal or extralegal, to regulate or suppress resources in libraries must be closely scrutinized to the end that protected expression is not abridged. Attempts to remove or suppress materials by library staff or members of the library's governing body that are not regulated or sanctioned by law are considered "extralegal." Examples include actions that circumvent library policy, or actions taken by elected officials or governing board members outside the established legal process for making legislative or board decisions. Actions taken by library governing bodies during official sessions or meetings pursuant to the library's collection development policy, or litigation undertaken in courts of law with jurisdiction over the library and the library's governing body, and actions taken by legislative bodies are considered a "legal process."

Content filtering is not equivalent to collection development. Content filtering is exclusive, not inclusive, and cannot effectively curate content or mediate access to resources available on the internet. Filtering should be addressed in an institution's policy on acceptable use of the internet. Acceptable use policies should reflect the *Library Bill of Rights* and "Internet Filtering: An Interpretation of the *Library Bill of Rights*," and be approved by the appropriate governing authority.

NOTES

1. "Libraries: An American Value," adopted February 3, 1999, by the ALA Council.

2. "Diversity in Collection Development: An Interpretation of the *Library Bill of Rights*," adopted July 14, 1982, by the ALA Council; amended January 10, 1990; July 2, 2008; and July 1, 2014. Revisions proposed January 2019.
3. "Access to Library Resources and Services for Minors: An Interpretation of the *Library Bill of Rights*," adopted June 30, 1972, by the ALA Council; amended July 1, 1981; July 3, 1991; June 30, 2004; July 2, 2008 under previous name "Free Access to Libraries for Minors"; and July 1, 2014.
4. *Bantam Books, Inc. v. Sullivan*, 372 U.S. 58 (1963).

Adopted June 25, 1971, by the ALA Council; amended July 1, 1981; January 10, 1990; January 28, 2009; July 1, 2014; January 29, 2019.

APPENDIX

Education and Information Literacy

An Interpretation of the Library Bill of Rights

Education and information literacy is fundamental to the mission of libraries of all types and the foundation for intellectual freedom. Intellectual freedom is the right of every individual to both seek and receive information from all points of view without restriction. Libraries provide access to information and ideas through their facilities, resources, and services. Libraries foster the ability to use those resources through educational programs and instruction.

The value and importance of intellectual freedom and its relationship to education is widely recognized in the Universal Declaration of Human Rights adopted by the United Nations in 1948. These principles are in strong alignment with the American Library Association's *Library Bill of Rights*.

The importance of intellectual freedom is expressed in both documents, and the necessity of education to the development of intellectual freedom is specifically discussed in Article 26 of the Universal Declaration of Human Rights:

> I. Everyone has the right to education. Education shall be free, at least in the elementary and fundamental stages.
> II. Education shall be directed to the full development of the human personality and to the strengthening of respect for human rights and fundamental freedoms. It shall promote understanding, tolerance and friendship among all nations, racial, or religious groups, and

shall further the activities of the United Nations for the maintenance of peace.[1]

The *Library Bill of Rights* "affirms that all libraries are forums for information and ideas," making them resources for facilitating education, developing curiosity, seeking knowledge, and further expanding the principles of intellectual freedom.

Access to information reflecting a variety of viewpoints is listed as the first principle in Article I:

> Books and other library resources should be provided for the interest, information, and enlightenment of all people of the community the library serves. Materials should not be excluded because of the origin, background, or views of those contributing to their creation.

Article II of the *Library Bill of Rights* emphasizes the importance of fostering access to information by providing materials that allow users to evaluate content and context and to find information representing multiple viewpoints:

Libraries should provide materials and information presenting all points of view on current and historical issues. Materials should not be proscribed or removed because of partisan or doctrinal disapproval.

Libraries and library workers foster education and lifelong learning by promoting free expression and facilitating the exchange of ideas between users. Libraries use resources, programming, and services to strengthen access to information and thus build a foundation of intellectual freedom. In their roles as educators, library workers create an environment that nurtures intellectual freedom in all library resources and services by:

- developing collections and services with multiple perspectives that empower individuals in the pursuit of their own interests
- providing programming that strengthens multiple methods of learning and expands opportunities to discover and respond to ideas
- leading instruction framed around information literacy skills and critical thinking
- advocating for the love of reading diverse voices and using the library to explore unfamiliar or controversial concepts

Through engaging in these educational services, libraries empower individuals to explore ideas, access and evaluate information, draw meaning from information presented in a variety of formats, develop valid conclusions, and express new ideas. Such endeavors facilitate access to information and offer a path to a robust appreciation of intellectual freedom rights and the value of libraries as cornerstones of the communities they serve.

NOTE
1. Universal Declaration of Human Rights, Article 26, United Nations General Assembly, December 10, 1948.

Adopted July 15, 2009, by the ALA Council under previous name "Importance of Education to Intellectual Freedom"; amended July 1, 2014 under previous name "Advocating for Intellectual Freedom"; revisions proposed and pending formal adoption as of March 2019.

APPENDIX

Equity, Diversity, Inclusion
An Interpretation of the Library Bill of Rights

The American Library Association affirms that equity, diversity, and inclusion are central to the promotion and practice of intellectual freedom. Libraries are essential to democracy and self-government, to personal development and social progress, and to every individual's inalienable right to life, liberty, and the pursuit of happiness. To that end, libraries and library workers should embrace equity, diversity, and inclusion in everything that they do.

"Equity" takes difference into account to ensure a fair process and, ultimately, a fair outcome. Equity recognizes that some groups were (and are) disadvantaged in accessing educational and employment opportunities and are, therefore, underrepresented or marginalized in many organizations and institutions. Equity, therefore, means increasing diversity by ameliorating conditions of disadvantaged groups.

"Diversity" can be defined as the sum of the ways that people are both alike and different. When we recognize, value, and embrace diversity, we are recognizing, valuing, and embracing the uniqueness of each individual.

"Inclusion" means an environment in which all individuals are treated fairly and respectfully; are valued for their distinctive skills, experiences, and perspectives; have equal access to resources and opportunities; and can contribute fully to the organization's success.

To ensure that every individual will feel truly welcomed and included, library staff and administrators should reflect the origins, age, background, and views of their community. Governing bodies should also reflect the community. Library spaces, programs, and collections should accommodate the needs of every user.

> I. Books and other library resources should be provided for the interest, information, and enlightenment of all people of the community the library serves. Materials should not be excluded because of the origin, age, background, or views of those contributing to their creation.
>
> Library collections, in a variety of material formats, should include a full range of viewpoints and experiences, serving the needs of all members of the community. Historically, diverse authors and viewpoints have not been equitably represented in the output of many mainstream publishers and other producers. It may require extra effort to locate, review, and acquire those materials.
>
> Therefore, libraries should seek out alternative, small press, independent, and self-published content in a variety of formats. Libraries may benefit from cooperative arrangements and other partnerships to share in the work of locating and acquiring diverse materials. Interlibrary loan may complement but not substitute for the development of diverse local collections.
>
> All materials, including databases and other electronic content, should be made accessible for people who use adaptive or assistive technology.
>
> To provide equitable and inclusive access, libraries must work closely with diverse communities to understand their needs and aspirations, so that the library can respond appropriately with collections and services to meet those needs. All community members will feel truly welcomed and included when they see themselves reflected in collections that speak to their cultures and life experiences.
>
> II. Libraries should provide materials and information presenting all points of view on current and historical issues. Materials should not be proscribed or removed because of partisan or doctrinal disapproval.
>
> Beyond merely avoiding the exclusion of materials representing unorthodox or unpopular ideas, libraries should proactively seek to

include an abundance of resources and programming representing the greatest possible diversity of genres, ideas, and expressions. A full commitment to equity, diversity, and inclusion requires that library collections and programming reflect the broad range of viewpoints and cultures that exist in our world. Socially excluded, marginalized, and underrepresented people, not just the mainstream majority, should be able to see themselves reflected in the resources and programs that libraries offer.[1]

III. Libraries should challenge censorship in the fulfillment of their responsibility to provide information and enlightenment.

By challenging censorship, libraries foster an inclusive environment where all voices have the opportunity to be heard. Inclusive materials, programs, and services may not be universally popular, but it is the library's responsibility to provide access to all points of view, not just prevailing opinions. Libraries should prepare themselves to deal with challenges by adopting appropriate policies and procedures. Libraries should respectfully consider community objections and complaints, but should not allow controversy alone to dictate policy.

Governing bodies, administrators, and library workers must discourage self-censorship. Fears and biases may suppress diverse voices in collections, programming, and all aspects of library services.[2] Libraries should counter censorship by practicing inclusion.

IV. Libraries should cooperate with all persons and groups concerned with resisting abridgment of free expression and free access to ideas.

American society has always encompassed people of diverse origin, age, background, and views. The constitutional principles of free expression and free access to ideas recognize and affirm this diversity. Any attempt to limit free expression or restrict access to ideas threatens the core American values of equity, diversity, and inclusion.

Libraries should establish and maintain strong ties to organizations that advocate for the rights of socially excluded, marginalized, and underrepresented people. Libraries should act in solidarity with all groups or individuals resisting attempts to abridge the rights of free expression and free access to ideas.

V. A person's right to use a library should not be denied or abridged because of origin, age, background, or views.

In the *Library Bill of Rights* and all of its Interpretations and supporting documents, the principle of inclusion is clear and unambiguous.

"Origin" encompasses all of the characteristics of individuals that are inherent in the circumstances of their birth.

"Age" encompasses all of the characteristics of individuals that are inherent in their levels of development and maturity.

"Background" encompasses all of the characteristics of individuals that are a result of their life experiences.

"Views" encompass all of the opinions and beliefs held and expressed by individuals.

Libraries should regularly review their policies with the goal of advancing equity of access to the library's collections and services. Identification requirements, overdue charges and fees, or deposits for service are examples of traditional approaches that may exclude some members of the community.[3]

VI. Libraries which make exhibit spaces and meeting rooms available to the public they serve should make such facilities available on an equitable basis, regardless of the beliefs or affiliations of individuals or groups requesting their use.

Libraries should not merely be neutral places for people to share information, but should actively encourage socially excluded, marginalized, and underrepresented people to fully participate in community debates and discussions.

Libraries should welcome diverse content in their exhibit spaces and diverse ideas, individuals, and groups in their meeting rooms, even if some members of the community may object or be offended.[4]

Conclusion

To uphold the *Library Bill of Rights* and serve the entire community, governing bodies, administrators, and library workers should embrace equity, diversity, and inclusion.

NOTES
1. "Library-Initiated Programs as a Resource: An Interpretation of the *Library Bill of Rights*," adopted January 27, 1982, by the ALA Council; amended June 26, 1990; July 12, 2000; June 26, 2018.
2. "Diversity in Collection Development: An Interpretation of the *Library Bill of Rights*," adopted July 14, 1982, by the ALA Council; amended January 10, 1990; July 2, 2008; July 1, 2014.
3. "Economic Barriers to Information Access: An Interpretation of the *Library Bill of Rights*," adopted June 30, 1993, by the ALA Council.
4. "Meeting Rooms: An Interpretation of the *Library Bill of Rights*," adopted July 2, 1991, by the ALA Council; Amended June 26, 2018; amended version rescinded August 16, 2018; amended January 29, 2019.

Adopted June 27, 2017, by the ALA Council.

APPENDIX

Exhibit Spaces and Bulletin Boards

An Interpretation of the Library Bill of Rights

Libraries often provide exhibit spaces and bulletin boards in physical and/or electronic formats. The uses made of these spaces should conform to the American Library Association's *Library Bill of Rights*: Article I states, "Materials should not be excluded because of the origin, background, or views of those contributing to their creation." Article II states, "Materials should not be proscribed or removed because of partisan or doctrinal disapproval." Article VI maintains that exhibit space should be made available "on an equitable basis, regardless of the beliefs or affiliations of individuals or groups requesting their use."

In developing library exhibits, staff members should endeavor to present a broad spectrum of opinion and a variety of viewpoints. Libraries should not shrink from developing exhibits because of controversial content or because of the beliefs or affiliations of those whose work is represented. Just as libraries do not endorse the viewpoints of those whose work is represented in their collections, libraries also do not endorse the beliefs or viewpoints of topics that may be the subject of library exhibits.

Exhibit areas often are made available for use by community groups. Libraries should formulate a written policy for the use of these exhibit areas to assure that space is provided on an equitable basis to all groups that request it. Written policies for exhibit space use should be stated in inclusive rather than exclusive terms. For example, a policy that the library's exhibit space is open "to organizations engaged in educational, cultural, intellectual, or charitable activities" is an inclusive statement of the limited uses of the exhibit space. This defined limitation would permit religious groups to use the exhibit space because they engage in intellectual activities, but would exclude most commercial uses of the exhibit space.

A publicly supported library may designate use of exhibit space for strictly library-related activities, provided that this limitation is viewpoint neutral and clearly defined.

Libraries may include in this policy rules regarding the time, place, and manner of use of the exhibit space, so long as the rules are content neutral and are applied in the same manner to all groups wishing to use the space. A library may wish to limit access to exhibit space to groups within the community served by the library. This practice is acceptable provided that the same rules and regulations apply to everyone, and that exclusion is not made on the basis of the doctrinal, religious, or political beliefs of the potential users.

The library should not censor or remove an exhibit because some members of the community may disagree with its content. Those who object to the content of any exhibit held at the library should be able to submit their complaint and/or their own exhibit proposal to be judged according to the policies established by the library.

Libraries may wish to post a permanent notice near the exhibit area stating that the library does not advocate or endorse the viewpoints of exhibits or exhibitors.

Libraries that make bulletin boards available to public groups for posting notices of public interest should develop criteria for the use of these spaces based on the same considerations as those outlined above. Libraries may wish to develop criteria regarding the size of material to be displayed, the length of time materials may remain on the bulletin board, the frequency with which material may be posted for the same group, and the geographic area from which notices will be accepted.

Adopted July 2, 1991, by the ALA Council; amended June 30, 2004; and July 1, 2014.

APPENDIX

Library-Initiated Programs as a Resource

An Interpretation of the Library Bill of Rights

Library-initiated programs support the mission of the library by providing users with additional opportunities for accessing information, education, and recreation. Article I of the *Library Bill of Rights* states, "Books and other library resources should be provided for the interest, information, and enlightenment of all people of the community the library serves."

Library-initiated programs utilize library staff expertise about community interests, collections, services, and facilities to provide access to information and information resources. Library-initiated programs introduce users and potential users to library resources and the library's role as a facilitator of information access. The library may participate in cooperative or joint programs with other agencies, organizations, institutions, or individuals to facilitate information access in the community the library serves.

Library-initiated programs include, but are not limited to, lectures, community forums, performing and visual arts,[1] participatory workshops, technology programming, creative learning programming, wellness programs, storytimes, continuing education, fairs and conventions, book clubs, discussion groups, demonstrations, displays, and presentations for social, cultural, educational, or entertainment purposes. Library-initiated programs may take place on-site at the library, off-site in other locations, or online and may be delivered by library staff, library volunteers, or library partners.

Libraries should not discriminate against individuals with disabilities and shall ensure they have equal access to library resources.[2] Library-initiated programs should comply with all applicable laws, including the standards and requirements of ADA and state or local disability accessibility guidelines. If a program is held in a location not controlled by the library, the library should assure that the space is accessible to all library users. If users overflow designated event areas during library events, libraries should protect accessible public spaces (i.e., ramps, pathways, and emergency exit routes) to ensure access and safety for everyone. Reasonable accommodations should also be made to have interpretation or real-time captioning for the deaf or hard-of hearing at library-initiated programs when needed or requested by library users.

As stated in "Equity, Diversity, Inclusion: An Interpretation of the *Library Bill of Rights*," "Socially excluded, marginalized and underrepresented people, not just the mainstream majority, should be able to see themselves reflected in the resources and programs that libraries offer."[3] Libraries should actively seek to include a variety of programming options representing diversity of genres, formats, ideas, and expressions with a multitude of viewpoints and cultural perspectives that reflect the diversity in our communities. Library-initiated programs that cross language and cultural barriers introduce underserved populations to the library's resources and provide access to information. Libraries serving multilingual or multicultural communities should make efforts to accommodate the information needs of those who speak and read languages other than English.

Libraries should have a policy guiding the development and implementation of programs, similar to material selection and building use policies, which has been approved by their policy-making body after consultation with legal counsel. These guidelines should set forth the library's commitment to free and open access to information and ideas for all users. Article II of the *Library Bill of Rights* states, "Materials should not be proscribed or removed because of partisan or doctrinal disapproval." Likewise, programs should not be canceled because of the ideas or topics of the program or the views expressed by the participants or speakers.[4] Library sponsorship of a program does not constitute an endorsement of the program content or the views expressed by the participants or speakers, any more than the purchase of material for the library collection constitutes an endorsement of the material content or its creator's views.

Libraries should vigorously defend the First Amendment right of speakers and participants to express themselves. Concerns, questions, or complaints about library-initiated programs are handled according to the same written policy and procedures that govern reconsiderations of other library resources.

Article V of the *Library Bill of Rights* states, "A person's right to use a library should not be denied or abridged because of origin, age, background, or views." The "right to use a library" encompasses all the resources the library offers, including the right to attend library-initiated programs. Libraries create programs for an intended age group or audience based on educational suitability and audience interest; however, restrictions on participation based solely on the gender, chronological age or educational level of users violates this right and should be enforced only when it would adversely impact the safety of the participants. Parents and guardians may restrict their own children's access to library programs, but no person or organization can interfere in others' access and participation.

Libraries should not deny access to library-initiated programs if patrons owe the library for overdue fines or other fees, nor should program attendees be required to share their personal information in order to attend a library program. Any collection of program participants' personal information should be on an opt-in basis only. If libraries charge program participants for supplies used, they should make every effort to reduce economic barriers to participation.

NOTES

1. "Visual and Performing Arts in Libraries: An Interpretation of the *Library Bill of Rights*," adopted February 13, 2018, by the ALA Council.
2. "Services to People with Disabilities: An Interpretation of the *Library Bill of Rights*," adopted January 28, 2009, by the ALA Council; amended June 26, 2018.
3. "Equity, Diversity, Inclusion: An Interpretation of the *Library Bill of Rights*," adopted June 27, 2017, by the ALA Council.
4. "Responding to and Preparing for Controversial Programs and Speakers Q&A," Intellectual Freedom Committee, June 2018.

Adopted January 27, 1982, by the ALA Council; amended June 26, 1990; July 12, 2000; June 26, 2018.

APPENDIX

Politics in American Libraries
An Interpretation of the Library Bill of Rights

The First Amendment to the United States Constitution states that "Congress shall make no law . . . abridging the freedom of speech, or of the press . . ." The *Library Bill of Rights* specifically states that "all people" and "all points of view" should be included in library materials and information. There are no limiting qualifiers for viewpoint, origin, or politics. Thus there is no justification for the exclusion of opinions deemed to be unpopular or offensive by some segments of society no matter how vocal or influential their opponents may be at any particular time in any particular place.

Associate Justice William J. Brennan, Jr. observed in *New York Times Co. v. Sullivan*, 376 U.S. 254 (1964), "[There exists a] profound national commitment to the principle that debate on public issues should be uninhibited, robust, and wide-open, and that it may well include vehement, caustic, and sometimes unpleasantly sharp attacks on government and public officials."

Therefore, libraries should collect, maintain, and provide access to as wide a selection of materials, reflecting as wide a diversity of views on political topics as possible, within their budgetary constraints and local community needs. A balanced collection need not and cannot contain an equal number of resources representing every possible viewpoint on every issue. A balanced collection should include the variety of views that surround any given issue.[1]

If a library has designated a space for community use, it must make that space available to all community organizations and groups regardless of their views or affiliations.[2] Libraries should rely on appropriate time, place, and manner regulations to guarantee equitable access and to avoid misuse of library space. These may include regulations governing the frequency and length of meetings and penalties on disruptive behavior.[3] Libraries should establish similar regulations if they make library space available for public exhibits or the public distribution of literature.[4]

The robust exchange of ideas and opinions is fundamental to a healthy democracy. Providing free, unfettered access to those ideas and opinions is an essential characteristic of American libraries. Therefore, libraries should encourage political discourse as part of civic engagement in forums designated for that purpose. Libraries should not ignore or avoid political discourse for fear of causing offense or provoking controversy.

Special limitations may apply to workplace speech (including political advocacy) by library employees.[5] When libraries are used as polling places, state statute or local ordinance may mandate temporary time, place, and manner restrictions on the political expression of members of the public, poll workers, and library employees while polling places are open.

This interpretation is most clearly applicable to public libraries. School, academic, and private libraries, including those associated with religious institutions, should apply these guidelines as befits or conforms to their institutional mission.

NOTES

1. "Diversity in Collection Development: An Interpretation of the *Library Bill of Rights*," adopted July 14, 1982, by the ALA Council; amended January 10, 1990; amended July 2, 2008; amended July 1, 2014.
2. "Meeting Rooms: An Interpretation of the *Library Bill of Rights*," adopted July 2, 1991, by the ALA Council.
3. "Guidelines for the Development of Policies and Procedures Regarding User Behavior and Library Usage," adopted January 24, 1993, by the Intellectual Freedom Committee; revised November 17, 2000; revised January 19, 2005; and March 29, 2014.
4. "Exhibit Spaces and Bulletin Boards: An Interpretation of the *Library Bill of Rights*," adopted July 2, 1991, by the ALA Council; amended June 30, 2004; and July 1, 2014.

5. "Speech in the Workplace Q&A," adopted by the Committee on Professional Ethics, July 2001; amended January 2004; amended June 26, 2006; amended January 24, 2007; amended July 1, 2014.

Endorsed by the ACRL Professional Values Committee in June 2017. Adopted June 27, 2017, by the ALA Council.

APPENDIX

The Universal Right to Free Expression

An Interpretation of the Library Bill of Rights

Freedom of expression is an inalienable human right and the foundation for self-government. Freedom of expression encompasses the freedoms of speech, press, religion, assembly, and association, and the corollary right to receive information without interference and without compromising personal privacy.

The American Library Association endorses this principle, which is also set forth in the Universal Declaration of Human Rights, adopted by the United Nations General Assembly. The Preamble of this document states that " . . . recognition of the inherent dignity and of the equal and inalienable rights of all members of the human family is the foundation of freedom, justice, and peace in the world . . ." and " . . . the advent of a world in which human beings shall enjoy freedom of speech and belief and freedom from fear and want has been proclaimed as the highest aspiration of the common people. . . ."

Article 12 of this document states:

> No one shall be subjected to arbitrary interference with his privacy, family, home or correspondence, nor to attacks upon his honor or reputation. Everyone has the right to the protection of the law against such interference or attacks.

Article 18 of this document states:

> Everyone has the right to freedom of thought, conscience and religion; this right includes freedom to change his religion or belief, and freedom, either alone or in community with others and in public or private, to manifest his religion or belief in teaching, practice, worship and observance.

Article 19 states:

> Everyone has the right to freedom of opinion and expression; this right includes freedom to hold opinions without interference and to seek, receive and impart information and ideas through any media regardless of frontiers.

Article 20 states:

> 1. Everyone has the right to freedom of peaceful assembly and association.
> 2. No one may be compelled to belong to an association.

On December 18, 2013, the United Nations General Assembly adopted a resolution reaffirming that the right to personal privacy applies to the use of communications technology and digital records, and requiring the governments of member nations to "respect and protect" the privacy rights of individuals.

We affirm our belief that these are inalienable rights of every person, regardless of origin, age, background, or views. We embody our professional commitment to these principles in the *Library Bill of Rights* and *Code of Ethics*, as adopted by the American Library Association.

We maintain that these are universal principles and should be applied by libraries and librarians throughout the world. The American Library Association's policy on International Relations reflects these objectives: ". . . to encourage the exchange, dissemination, and access to information and the unrestricted flow of library materials in all formats throughout the world."

We know that censorship, ignorance, and manipulation are the tools of tyrants and profiteers. We support the principles of Net neutrality, transparency, and accountability. We maintain that both government and corporate efforts to suppress, manipulate, or intercept personal communications and search queries with minimal oversight or accountability, and without user consent, is oppressive and discriminatory. The technological ability of commercial and government interests to engage in the massive collection and aggregation of personally identifiable information without due process and transparency is an abuse of the public trust and inimical to privacy and free expression. We believe that everyone benefits when each individual is treated with respect, and ideas and information are freely shared, openly debated, and vigorously tested in the market of public experience.

The American Library Association is unswerving in its commitment to human rights, but cherishes a particular commitment to privacy and free expression; the two are inseparably linked and inextricably entwined with the professional practice of librarianship. We believe that the rights of privacy and free expression are not derived from any claim of political, racial, economic, or cultural hegemony. These rights are inherent in every individual. They cannot be surrendered or subordinated, nor can they be denied, by the decree of any government or corporate interest. True justice and equality depend upon the constant exercise of these rights.

We recognize the power of information and ideas to inspire justice, to restore freedom and dignity to the exploited and oppressed, to change the hearts and minds of the oppressors, and to offer opportunities for a better life to all people.

Courageous people, in difficult and dangerous circumstances throughout human history, have demonstrated that freedom lives in the human heart and cries out for justice even in the face of threats, enslavement, imprisonment, torture, exile, and death. We draw inspiration from their example. They challenge us to remain steadfast in our most basic professional responsibility to promote and defend the rights of privacy and free expression.

There is no good censorship. Any effort to restrict free expression and the free flow of information through any media and regardless of frontiers aids discrimination and oppression. Fighting oppression with censorship is self-defeating. There is no meaningful freedom for the individual without personal privacy. A society that does not respect the privacy of the individual will be blind to the erosion of its rights and liberties.

Threats to the privacy and freedom of expression of any person anywhere are threats to the privacy and freedom of all people everywhere. Violations of these human rights have been recorded in virtually every country and society across the globe. Vigilance in protecting these rights is our best defense.

In response to these violations, we affirm these principles:

> The American Library Association opposes any use of governmental prerogative that leads to intimidation of individuals that prevents them from exercising their rights to hold opinions without interference, and to seek, receive, and impart information and ideas. We urge libraries and librarians everywhere to resist such abuse of governmental power, and to support those against whom such governmental power has been employed.

The American Library Association condemns any governmental effort to involve libraries and librarians in restrictions on the right of any individual to hold opinions without interference, and to seek, receive, and impart information and ideas. Such restrictions, whether enforced by statutes or regulations, contractual stipulations, or voluntary agreements, pervert the function of the library and violate the professional responsibilities of librarians.

The American Library Association rejects censorship in any form. Any action that denies the inalienable human rights of individuals only damages the will to resist oppression, strengthens the hand of the oppressor, and undermines the cause of justice.

The American Library Association will not abrogate these principles. We believe that censorship corrupts the cause of justice, and contributes to the demise of freedom.

Adopted January 16, 1991, by the ALA Council; amended on July 1, 2014.

APPENDIX

Visual and Performing Arts in Libraries

An Interpretation of the Library Bill of Rights

Visual and performing arts can transform understanding and appreciation of the world in all its cultural diversity. The American Library Association affirms that visual and performing arts can be powerful components of library collections and services. The arts play a vital role in our ability to communicate a broad spectrum of ideas to all people. Developing an understanding and appreciation of visual and performing arts promotes artistic literacy. Libraries should offer opportunities for the community to experience art.

Art can serve personal, political, and aesthetic functions, including personal expression, and social, historical, or political messaging. It may enhance day-to-day living, create visual delight, or challenge the status quo. For the purposes of this interpretation of the *Library Bill of Rights*, art is defined as work created or designated by an artist, with the ability to provoke an aesthetic response, or affect the human senses in some way. Ultimately art is a product combining the artist's creativity, the viewer's perception, and a representation of the culture and time in which the work was produced.

Visual art is created with the implication of human manufacture. Visual art includes but is not limited to painting, sculpture, photography, design, digital, fiber, and decorative arts involving a wide variety of visual media. Visual art has visible properties (whether or not it is seen) and there are always some aspects of the formal elements of art—line, shape, color, form, texture, etc. Performance art is defined as physical movement, placement, or theatrical activity involving people in defined space, with the explicit or implicit application of artistic direction, choreography, curatorial planning, or design. Performance art may include aspects or elements of music, dance, mime, and acting, with attributes of professional or amateur stagecraft. As with the visual arts, performance art may either confirm or challenge cultural familiarity, and as stated in Article I of the *Library Bill of Rights*, contributes to the "interest, information, and enlightenment of all people of the community the library serves."[1]

Libraries may choose to provide both physical and virtual spaces for the community to experience and interact with artistic content and programs or to create their own art. Works of visual and performing art may be temporary exhibits, permanent installations, programs or performances offered in the library, or parts of a library's viewable or archived collections.

In developing library arts exhibits and programs, libraries should present a broad spectrum of opinions and viewpoints as codified in the *Library Bill of Rights*, Articles I and II. Libraries should not avoid developing exhibits or programs because of controversial content, or because of the beliefs or affiliations of those whose work is represented. Libraries do not endorse the viewpoints of the artists themselves, the artwork owners, or the exhibit organizers, whether or not they are internal or external contributors to library programs and collections.[2]

Libraries that choose to make gallery or performing space available for use by community groups or individuals should formulate a written policy for the use of these areas and may adopt time, place, and manner rules for such use. Libraries may wish to develop such criteria as the size of the artwork to be displayed, space requirements including for an audience, the length of time the work may remain on display or in performance, the frequency with which material may be displayed from the same group, or whether to accept work only from local constituents or stakeholders.

Such policies should also ensure that space is provided on an equitable basis to all who request it and should be stated in inclusive rather than exclusive terms. Policies and publicity should be written to encourage use of library public display, exhibit, and performance spaces by a broad range of organizations and individuals.[3]

However, as with any meeting space, a publicly funded library may instead choose to restrict use of display, exhibit, and performance spaces to "strictly 'library-related activities' provided that the limitation is clearly circumscribed and is viewpoint neutral."[4]

The library's policies for arts programming and exhibits should be readily available to the public. Behavior policies should not be used to limit access to art or performances in the library. If users object to a particular work of art or performance there should be a method of recourse, similar to a reconsideration policy, for expressing their concerns.

All art in the library's permanent or exhibit holdings is an integral part of the library's collections just the same as literary, film, eBooks, and all other material types. Collection development policies should include the collection of, and access to, art where possible. The library should provide a welcoming and content-rich environment for all users to engage with visual art or to create their own projects. Libraries are encouraged to be intentional in including diverse voices, be it through creative projects, performances, or exhibits from many cultural traditions. When the library plans exhibitions or performances, the selection should consider all of the communities served and should provide diverse points of view.

State and federal law may mandate that libraries use internet filters.[5] Such filters may block moving and still images and can be especially problematic when users seek information on the visual arts. Library policy should therefore offer and encourage library users to ask for unfiltered access to websites, and for content to be unrestricted with due respect for user privacy. Libraries should consult the Internet Filtering interpretation[5] for more information on CIPA. There should be no barriers to child or teen access to visual and performing arts within the library.

In summary, visual images and performances in the library should not be restricted based on content. Librarians and library staff should be proactive in seeking out a wide variety of representational and abstract artwork and performance art, with limitations or parameters set only with respect to space, installation, fiscal, and technical constraints. The same criteria for access to literature of all kinds for all people are relevant to visual media and performing arts in libraries.

NOTES

1. *Library Bill of Rights*, adopted June 19, 1939, by the ALA Council; amended October 14, 1944; June 18, 1948; February 2, 1961; June 27, 1967; January 23, 1980; inclusion of "age" reaffirmed January 23, 1996.

2. "Politics in American Libraries: An Interpretation of the *Library Bill of Rights*," endorsed by the ACRL Professional Values Committee in June 2017; adopted June 27, 2017, by the ALA Council.
3. "Exhibit Spaces and Bulletin Boards: An Interpretation of the *Library Bill of Rights*," adopted July 2, 1991, by the ALA Council; amended June 30, 2004; and July 1, 2014.
4. "Meeting Rooms: An Interpretation of the *Library Bill of Rights*," adopted July 2, 1991, by the ALA Council; amended June 26, 2018; amended version rescinded August 16, 2018; amended January 29, 2019.
5. "Internet Filtering: An Interpretation of the *Library Bill of Rights*," adopted June 30, 2015, by the ALA Council.

Adopted February 13, 2018, by the ALA Council.

APPENDIX

Code of Ethics

As members of the American Library Association, we recognize the importance of codifying and making known to the profession and to the general public the ethical principles that guide the work of librarians, other professionals providing information services, library trustees and library staffs.

Ethical dilemmas occur when values are in conflict. The American Library Association Code of Ethics states the values to which we are committed, and embodies the ethical responsibilities of the profession in this changing information environment.

We significantly influence or control the selection, organization, preservation, and dissemination of information. In a political system grounded in an informed citizenry, we are members of a profession explicitly committed to intellectual freedom and the freedom of access to information. We have a special obligation to ensure the free flow of information and ideas to present and future generations.

The principles of this Code are expressed in broad statements to guide ethical decision making. These statements provide a framework; they cannot and do not dictate conduct to cover particular situations.

- We provide the highest level of service to all library users through appropriate and usefully organized resources; equitable service

policies; equitable access; and accurate, unbiased, and courteous responses to all requests.
- We uphold the principles of intellectual freedom and resist all efforts to censor library resources.
- We protect each library user's right to privacy and confidentiality with respect to information sought or received and resources consulted, borrowed, acquired or transmitted.
- We respect intellectual property rights and advocate balance between the interests of information users and rights holders.
- We treat co-workers and other colleagues with respect, fairness, and good faith, and advocate conditions of employment that safeguard the rights and welfare of all employees of our institutions.
- We do not advance private interests at the expense of library users, colleagues, or our employing institutions.
- We distinguish between our personal convictions and professional duties and do not allow our personal beliefs to interfere with fair representation of the aims of our institutions or the provision of access to their information resources.
- We strive for excellence in the profession by maintaining and enhancing our own knowledge and skills, by encouraging the professional development of co-workers, and by fostering the aspirations of potential members of the profession.

Adopted at the 1939 Midwinter Meeting by the ALA Council; amended June 30, 1981; June 28, 1995; and January 22, 2008.

INDEX

A
Abunimah, Ali, 35
academic freedom
   art censorship and, 16, 19
   ideals of, 57–58
   for librarians, 55
access
   to databases, 85
   decision to deny access to materials, 90
   to digital information, services, networks, 101–104
   equitable access to information, xiv–xv, 116
   equity of, 103
   free access to ideas, 117
   information resources and, 103–104
   intellectual freedom and, 112–114
   to library programs, 123, 124
   to library resources, 106–107
   to library space, 126
   rights of users, 102
"Access to Digital Information, Services, and Networks" (ALA), 85–86, 101–104
"Access to Library Resources and Services Regardless of Sex, Gender Identity, Gender Expression, or Sexual Orientation" (ALA), 106–108
accessibility, 123
Adler v. Board of Education, 58
Adult Programs in the Library (Lear), 30
African Americans, 16–18

age, 118
Akron-Summit County Public Library, Ohio, 35
Alaska Civil Liberties Union, 5–6
Albany Public Library, New York, 50
Amazon.com, 79
American Bar Association, 6–7
American Civil Liberties Union (ACLU), 19, 66
American Libraries, 31
American Library Association (ALA)
   "Access to Digital Information, Services, and Networks," 101–104
   "Access to Library Resources and Services Regardless of Sex, Gender Identity, Gender Expression, or Sexual Orientation," 106–108
   on Arizona's book restrictions, 54
   books on social media published by, 63
   censorship reports to, 91–93, 95–96
   "Challenged Resources" (ALA), 109–111
   Code of Ethics, 23, 136–137
   on databases, protection of, 85–86
   "Declaration for the Right to Libraries," 55
   on "Dirty Dozen List," 79
   "Education and Information Literacy," 56, 112–114
   "Equity, Diversity, Inclusion," 115–119
   "Exhibit Spaces and Bulletin Boards," 7–8, 120–121

139

American Library Association (ALA) *(cont'd)*
  Library Bill of Rights, 99
  "Library-Initiated Programs as a Resource," 122–124
  policy on meeting rooms, viii
  "Politics in American Libraries," 126–127
  on programs, 39
  reporting challenges to, 89–90
  silent censorship and, 94–95
  "Social Media Guidelines for Public and Academic Libraries," 73–74
  social media, right to post/right to block, 68–69
  "The Universal Right to Free Expression," 128–131
  "Visual and Performing Arts in Libraries," 21–22, 132–134
  See also Office for Intellectual Freedom
An Unseen Angel: A Mother's Story of Faith, Hope and Healing after Sandy Hook (Parker), 9
Anchorage, Alaska, 5–6
appendices
  "Access to Digital Information, Services, and Networks" (ALA), 101–104
  "Access to Library Resources and Services Regardless of Sex, Gender Identity, Gender Expression, or Sexual Orientation" (ALA), 106–108
  "Challenged Resources" (ALA), 109–111
  "Code of Ethics" (ALA), 136–137
  "Education and Information Literacy" (ALA), 112–114
  "Equity, Diversity, Inclusion" (ALA), 115–119
  "Exhibit Spaces and Bulletin Boards" (ALA), 120–121
  Library Bill of Rights, 99
  "Library-Initiated Programs as a Resource" (ALA), 122–124
  "Politics in American Libraries" (ALA), 125–126
  "The Universal Right to Free Expression" (ALA), 128–131
  "Visual and Performing Arts in Libraries" (ALA), 132–134
Arce v. Douglas, 54
Arce v. Huppenthal, 54
Arizona House Bill 2281, 52–54
Arlington Heights Memorial Library, Illinois, 34
art
  censorship of, 15–19
  definition of, 132
  display policies, 22–24
  First Amendment protections, 19–21
  in libraries, 13–15
  poem, censorship of, 25–26
  procedures for, 24–25
  "Visual and Performing Arts in Libraries" (ALA), 21–22, 132–134
artists, 14–15
Artists Rights (National Coalition Against Censorship & Center for Democracy and Technology), 22
Asheim, Lester, 90–91
At-Risk Summer (documentary film), 31–32
The Audacity of Hope (Obama), 15–16
audiences, 73
Aurora Public Library, Illinois, 25–26
authority, 47
autonomy, 38
Ayers, Bill, 34
Ayers, Stephen, 17

B
background, 118
balance
  bias *vs.*, 40–41
  in *Code of Ethics* (ALA), 137
  Fairness Doctrine, 68
  library social media strategy and, 74
Ballard, Terry, 63
Baltimore, Maryland, 65–66
ban, 90
banned books
  in Arizona, 52–54
  censorship reports on, 92
Banned Books Week
  censorship of, vii–viii
  censorship of library display for, 6
  social media posts, censorship of, 65–66
Baton Rouge, Louisiana, 51–52
The Battle for Justice in Palestine (Abunimah), 35
Be a Hero! The Essential Survival Guide to Active-Shooter Events (Geddes), 9
bias
  balance *vs.*, 40–41
  social media and, 65
Bigelow, Bill, 52–53
Binghamton, New York, 32–33
Bitar, Samir, 31
Black History Month, 3
Blackmun, Harry, 37
blocking
  right to block, 67–69
  of social media users by elected officials, 66–67

Board of Education, Adler v., 58
Board of Trustees of University of Illinois, Snyder v., 37
book display, 1
bookmarks, 46
books
    banned books in Tucson, Arizona, 52–54
    Banned Books Week, censorship and, vii–viii
    book challenge case, ix–xii
    censorship reports on, 92
    displays of, 2
    for equity, diversity, inclusion, 116
    on social media, 63
    See also reading lists
Books, Blackboards, and Bullets: School Shootings and Violence in America (Lebrun), 9
Bowling for Columbine (Moore), 9
Bradley, Phil, 63
Brennan, William, Jr., 20, 125
Brewer, Jan, 52
Broome County Public Library, 32–33
Brown, Michael, 16–17
bulletin boards, 120–121
Bunker, Lisa, 50

C

Cacheris, James C., 66
California, Miller v., 82
Campbell, Wendy, 31
Capitol Hill, Washington, D. C., 16–17
Carlson, Jennifer, 9
Carlson, Liz, 10
Cary Memorial Library, Lexington, Massachusetts, 70–71
case studies
    artwork, censorship of, 16–19
    introduction to, xv–xvi
    library displays, censorship of, 4–6
    See also censorship
Castillo, Peter, 17
Cedar Creek School District, Colorado, 81
Celebrate Literacy Week, 51
censorship
    art display policies and, 22–24
    of artwork, 15–19
    Banned Books Week and, vii–viii
    of databases, 78–81
    of databases, protection against, 82–86
    LGBTQ book challenge case, ix–xii
    librarians and, xv–xvii
    library challenges of, 117
    of library displays, 4–6
    of programs/events, 30–35
    of reading lists, 47–54
    reporting, 89–95
    reporting, support for, 95–97
    of social media, 64–67
    "The Universal Right to Free Expression" (ALA), 129–131
Centennial, Colorado, 80–81
Center for Democracy and Technology, 22
"Challenged Resources" (ALA), 109–111
challenges
    art display policy on, 23–24
    of censorship by library, 117
    censorship reports, 89–95
    "Challenged Resources" (ALA), 109–111
    database subscribers, protection of, 82–86
    of databases, 78–81
    definition of, 89–90
    exhibit policy on procedure for, 8–9
    types of, xi
Charleston County Public Library, South Carolina, 4
Charlton-Trujillo, e.E., 31–32
Chbosky, Stephen, x, 48
Cherry Creek School District, Colorado, 79
Chicano! The History of the Mexican American Civil Rights Movement (Rosales), 52
Children's Internet Protection Act (CIPA), 81
Citizen-Protectors: The Everyday Politics of Guns in an Age of Decline (Carlson), 9
Clay, Lacy, 17
CLiC (Colorado Library Consortium), 80–81
"closed public forum," 36
Code of Ethics (ALA)
    art display policy and, 23
    copy of, 136–137
    on excellence in library profession, 57
collaboration, 14, 22
collection
    of art, 134
    for equity, diversity, inclusion, 116–117
Colorado Library Consortium (CLiC), 80–81
Columbine (Cullen), 9
The Columbine Shootings (Gimpel), 10
commercial speech, 7
Common (musician/rapper), 15–16
communication
    programming librarians and, 38
    social media, blocking, 68
    social media for, 61–64
community
    artwork partnerships with library, 14–15
    censorship reporting and, 96
    equity, diversity, inclusion at library, 115–118

142 | Index

community *(cont'd)*
    library exhibit areas, use of, 120–121
    library space for, 126
    social media for communication with, 61–64
complaints
    about art, 23–25
    about library displays, 3, 10
    about library exhibits, 121
    about reading lists, 47–54
    censorship of programs/events, 30–35
    exhibit policy on procedure for, 8–9
    See also challenges
Concerned Christian Citizens, 5
Concerned Citizens for School Databases, 79
confidentiality
    censorship reporting and, 95
    in *Code of Ethics* (ALA), 137
    users' right of, 102
connection, 45
constitutional protections
    See U.S. Constitution
content filtering, 85–86
controversial topics
    bias *vs.* balance, 40–41
    library programming on, 39
controversies, 64–67
    See also censorship; challenges
cooperation, 117
Crawford, Walt, 63
Creative Management of Small Public Libraries in the 21st Century (Harbeson), 1–2
criteria, for reading lists, 47
Critical Race Theory (Delgado), 52
Cullen, David, 9
current events, 9–10

D

Daily Herald, 34
D'Antuono, Michael, 17
Darby Public Library, Montana, 31
data, 91, 93
databases
    censorship of, viii
    challenges to, 86
    complaints about, 78–81
    overview of, 77–78
    right to reference, 81–82
    subscribers, saving, 82–86
Davison, Brian C., 67
Davison v. Loudoun County Board of Supervisors, 69
de la Peña, Matt, 53
debate, 125
decisions
    about access to digital information, 102
    censorship reports and, 91–92, 96
"Declaration for the Right to Libraries" (ALA), 55
Deering Library Reading Room, 14
Delgado, Rodolfo, 52
democracy, 96–97
Denver, Colorado
    censorship of art in, 17–18
    censorship of social media in, 64–65
Denver Police Protective Association, 18
The Denver Post, 18
Denver Public Schools (DPS), 17–18
"designated public forum," 36
Deuker, Carl, 51
digital resources
    access to, 101–104
    databases, 77–78, 85–86
directional aids, 46
"Dirty Dozen List," 78–79
display furniture, 2
displays/exhibits
    about current events, 9–10
    art display policies, 22–24
    artwork complemented by, 14
    censorship case studies, 4–6
    displays, defending, 7–9
    exhibits creators, educating, 10–11
    purposes/value of, 1–4
    right to showcase, 6–7
diversity
    balanced library collection, 125
    definition of, 115
    "Equity, Diversity, Inclusion" (ALA), 115–119
Doherty, Teresa, 74
Doing Social Media So It Matters: A Librarian's Guide (Solomon), 63
Douglas, Arce v., 54
Douglas, William O., 58
Drag Queen Story Time, 32–33
Duncan, Jim, 81

E

EBSCO
    challenges to, 83
    controversies over databases, 79–81
    on "Dirty Dozen List," 78–79
    right to reference, 81–82
    student access to, 86
Eby, Kermit, 34
education, 112–114
"Education and Information Literacy" (ALA), 56, 112–114
elected officials, 66–67, 69

Enoch Pratt Free Library, Baltimore, 4, 66
Enough: Our Fight to Keep America Safe from Gun Violence (Gifford), 9
equity
　definition of, 115
　equitable access to information, xiv–xv
　"Equity, Diversity, Inclusion" (ALA), 115–119
ethics
　Code of Ethics (ALA), 57, 136–137
　review of challenged resources, 23
Etingoff, Kim, 9
Evanston Public Library, Illinois, 35
events
　See programs/events
"Exhibit Spaces and Bulletin Boards" (ALA), 7–8, 120–121
exhibits
　availability of library exhibit spaces, 118
　definition of, 1
　educating exhibits creators, 10–11
　equitable access to, 107
　"Exhibit Spaces and Bulletin Boards" (ALA), 7–8, 120–121
　of visual/performing arts, 133–134
　See also displays/exhibits
The Exile: Sex, Drugs and Libel in the New Russia (Ames & Taibbi), 35
expression, freedom of
　academic freedom and, 55
　First Amendment protections, 19–21
　freedom of, 101
　right to speak/right to program, 36
　"The Universal Right to Free Expression" (ALA), 128–131

F
Facebook
　censorship of library programs on, 32, 33
　right to block, 69
　social media, censorship of, 67
Fairness Doctrine, 68
Family Watch International, 86
Fat Angie (Charlton-Trujillo), 31–32
fear, 58, 117
Federal Communications Commission, 67–68
feedback, 39
Felix Yz (Bunker), 50
First Amendment
　access to library resources and, 106, 107
　artwork, protections for, 19–21
　ban of materials, 90
　censorship reports and, 91, 92
　databases and, 81–82
　on library display, 5–6
　library programs and, 124
　politics in libraries and, 125–126
　right to showcase, 6–7
　right to speak/right to program, 37–38
　right to suggest, engage, teach, 54–55
　social media and, 64, 66, 68–69
500 Years of Chicano History in Pictures (Martinez), 52
Florida Department of Education, 51
Forbes Library, Northampton, Massachusetts, 8
Forbes Magazine, 61
forum, 106, 113
Frances & Taylor Group, 62
Franklin, Benjamin, 64
free speech
　"Access to Digital Information, Services, and Networks" (ALA), 101–104
　artwork, protections for, 19, 20
　Barack Obama on, 96–97
　censorship of social media, 64–67
　politics in libraries and, 125–126
　right to speak/right to program, 36–38
　social justice and, xiii–xiv
　"The Universal Right to Free Expression" (ALA), 128–131
freedom
　academic freedom, 16, 19, 57–58
　professional freedoms, 55–57
　See also expression, freedom of; intellectual freedom
Freedom to Read Foundation, 54
Freire, Paulo, 53

G
Gail Borden Public Library District, Illinois, 39
Gale-Cengage
　database controversy, 80
　pornography on databases, 79
　student access to, 86
Garnar, Martin, vii–viii, xiv
Garner, Eric, 35
Garst, Kim, 61
gay pride display, 5–6
Gay Straight Alliance (GSA), 47–49
Geddes, John, 9
gender identity/expression, 106–108
　See also LGBTQ; sexuality/sexual orientation
Geography Club (Hartinger), 48
George (Gino), 49–50
Gifford, Gabrielle, 9
Gimpel, Diane, 10

Gino, Alex, 49–50
Give a Boy a Gun (Strasser), 9
GLBT Book Month, 3, 4–5
Goggin, Brian, 14
Gonzales, Rodolfo, 52
Google This! Putting Google and Other Social Media Sites to Work for Your Library (Ballard), 63
government agencies, 66–67
Goya, Francisco, 17
graphic novels, 3
Greene, Rachel, 18
Gregg, Tom, 19
Grey, William, 18
GSA (Gay Straight Alliance), 47–49
Gun Control and the Second Amendment (Hand), 9
Gunman on Campus (Etingoff), 9
Gunned Down: The Power of the NRA (Kirk), 9
Gutless (Deuker), 51

H
Hand, Carol, 9
Harbeson, Cynthia, 1–2
Harold Washington Library, Illinois, 14
Hartinger, Brent, 48
Hennepin County Library, Minnesota, 22–23
"Hijab Means Jihad" (poem), 25–26
Hillsborough County Commission, 6
Hillsborough County, Florida, 6
Hispanic students, 52–54
historical events, 3
The History of the Mexican American Civil Rights Movement (Rosales), 53
Holtz, Shel, 73
Huppenthal, Arce v., 54
Hurston, Zora Neale, 77

I
I Can't Breathe (Taibbi), 35
ICE (U.S. Immigration and Customs Enforcement), 34
ideas, 126, 130
IFC (Intellectual Freedom Committee), 73–74
inclusion
  "Equity, Diversity, Inclusion" (ALA), 115–119
  exhibit areas policy and, 120–121
information
  equitable access to, xiv–xv
  right to receive, 20
information resources, 103–104
  See also digital resources

Institute of Museum and Library Services, 91–92
intellectual freedom
  academic freedom, ideals of, 57–58
  art display policies and, 23
  censorship and, viii
  censorship reporting, support for, 95–97
  in *Code of Ethics* (ALA), 136–137
  databases, reconsideration policies, 84–85
  "Education and Information Literacy" (ALA), 112–114
  equity, diversity, inclusion, 115–119
  LGBTQ book challenge case, ix–xii
  professional freedoms, 55–57
Intellectual Freedom Committee (IFC), 73–74
internet
  right to reference, 81–82
  single voice via, 74
  social media, right to post/right to block, 67–69
internet filtering
  access to visual/performing arts, 134
  ALA on, 81–82, 85–86, 104
"Internet Filtering" (ALA), 85–86
internet service providers, 67
Islam, 31
It (King), 3
Itatani, Michiko, 14

J
Jay High School, Santa Rosa County, Florida, 51
Jefferson County Public Library, Colorado, 64–65
Jewish Community Foundation of Greater Kansas City, 33
Johannesburg, South Africa, 67
John, Elton, 62
Johnson, Lyndon, 13
Jones, Barbara
  on *Arce v. Huppenthal*, 54
  Kristin Pekoll and, xii, xvi
  "Visual and Performing Arts in Libraries," 21–22
Journal of Intellectual Freedom and Privacy, 83–84

K
Kansas City Public Library, Missouri, 33, 71–72
Kemper, Crosby, III, 33
Kennedy, Anthony, 68–69, 74
King, David Lee, 63

King, Stephen, 3
Kirk, Michael, 9
Klebold, Sue, 9
Kleindienst, Richard, 37
Kleindienst v. Mandel, 37
"Know Your Rights" event, 34
Knowlton, Stephen, 51
Krug, Judith, xvi-xvii
Ku Klux Klan, 17, 18

L

Lafayette Library, California, 14
Lake Oswego School District, 49-50
Lamont v. Postmaster General, 20
LaRue, Jamie
   on censorship, 89
   on EBSCO, 83-84
   Kristin Pekoll and, xii, xvi
   on tweets, 65
law enforcement
   art portraying police officers, 16-18
   censorship of library events and, 33, 34
   Stonewall riots, 5
Lear, Brett, 30
learning
   First Amendment protections, 54-55
   professional freedoms, 55-57
Lebrun, Marcel, 9
legal defenses
   See rights; U.S. Constitution
LGBTQ
   "Access to Library Resources and Services Regardless of Sex, Gender Identity, Gender Expression, or Sexual Orientation" (ALA), 106-108
   book challenge case, ix-xii
   censorship of library displays, 4-6
   censorship of programs/events, 30-33
   databases, challenges of, 86
   reading lists, censorship of, 47-50
librarians
   academic freedom, ideals of, 57-58
   censorship reporting, professional support for, 95-97
   censorship reports by, 92, 94-95
   challenges, xi
   Code of Ethics (ALA), 136-137
   displays, educating about, 10-11
   engagement with communities, xiv
   equitable access to information, xiv-xv
   "Equity, Diversity, Inclusion" (ALA), 115-119
   library displays and, 3-4
   professional freedoms, 55-57
   programming librarians, 30, 38-40
   reading list by, 45-47
   reading lists, censorship of, 47-54
   right to suggest, engage, teach, 54-55
   rights of, defense of, xv
   social media managers, 69-74
   social media use by, 61-64
The Librarian's Nitty-Gritty Guide to Social Media (Solomon), 63
libraries
   academic freedom, ideals of, 57-58
   access to library resources, 106-107
   art display policies of, 22-24
   artwork, protection of, 21-22
   artwork in, 13-15
   challenged resources, 109-111
   displays, defending, 7-9
   "Education and Information Literacy" (ALA), 112-114
   "Equity, Diversity, Inclusion" (ALA), 115-119
   "Politics in American Libraries" (ALA), 125-126
   programming librarians, 38-40
   programming policies of, 40-41
   programs as essential service for everyone, 29-30
   right to speak/right to program, 36-38
   roles of, xiv
   social media for community communication, 61-64
   social media policy, 70-73
   social media, training for, 69-70
   "Visual and Performing Arts in Libraries" (ALA), 132-134
Library Bill of Rights (ALA)
   "Access to Digital Information, Services, and Networks," 101-104
   "Access to Library Resources and Services Regardless of Sex, Gender Identity, Gender Expression, or Sexual Orientation," 106-108
   "Challenged Resources," 109-111
   copy of, 99
   databases, interpretations about, 85-86
   displays interpretation, 7-8
   "Education and Information Literacy," 56, 112-114
   "Equity, Diversity, Inclusion," 115-119
   "Exhibit Spaces and Bulletin Boards," 120-121
   "Library-Initiated Programs as a Resource," 122-124
   "Politics in American Libraries," 125-126
   programs interpretation, 39
   on reporting censorship, 94

Library Bill of Rights (ALA) *(cont'd)*
  "The Universal Right to Free Expression," 128–131
  "Visual and Performing Arts in Libraries," 21–22, 132–134
Library Marketing and Communications Conference, 73
Library Services and Technology Act, 81–82
library staff
  social media training for, 69–70
  social media use by, 61–64
  See also librarians
"Library-Initiated Programs as a Resource" (ALA), 39
Librotraficantes, 54
Lieberman, Joseph, 9
"limited public forum," 36
London, Scott, 18
Lopez, Rafael, 14
Loudoun County Board of Supervisors, Davison v., 69
Louisiana Center for the Book, State Library of Louisiana, 51–52
Louisiana Teen Readers' Choice program, 51–52

M
Macintyre, Ben, 29
Madison Public Library, Wisconsin, 23
Managing Your Library's Social Media Channels (King), 63
Mandel, Ernest, 37
Mandel, Kleindienst v. Mandel, 37
marketing, 62
Marketing and Social Media: A Guide for Libraries, Archives, and Museums (Thomsett-Scott), 63
Marshall, Thurgood, 37
Martinez, Elizabeth, 52
Maycock, Angela, x
meeting rooms, 118
Menomonie, Wisconsin, 16
Men's Health, 79
Message to Aztlán: Selected Writings of Rodolfo "Corky" Gonzalez (Gonzales), 52
Mexican American Studies (MAS) program, 52–54
Mexican WhiteBoy (de la Peña), 53
Meyer, Bob, 16
Midlothian Public Library, Illinois, 41
Miller v. California, 82
Mintcheva, Svetlana, 18
Mombian (blog), 6
Moore, Michael, 9

"The Moral Arc of History Ideally Bends towards Justice, but Just as Soon as Not Curves Back around toward Barbarism, Sadism, and Unrestrained Chaos" (Walker), 18
A Mother's Reckoning: Living in the Aftermath of Tragedy (Klebold), 9
Murfreesboro, Tennessee, 20–21

N
Naperville North High School, Illinois, 34
National Center on Sexual Exploitation (NCOSE), 78–79, 86
National Coalition Against Censorship
  Artist Rights resource, 22
  letter to Bob Meyer, 16
  library art display guidance, 22
National Latino Police Officers Association, 18
Neal, Diane Rasmussen, 63
New York, 50
New York Times Co. v. Sullivan, 125
New Yorker's Family Research Foundation, 33
Newark Public Library, New Jersey, 18
Nineteen Minutes (Picoult), 9
Norfolk Public Library, Virginia, 8–9
North Carolina, Packingham v., 68–69, 74
"Not Censorship but Selection" (Asheim), 90–91
The NRA Step-by-Step Guide to Gun Safety: How to Safely Care for, Use, and Store Your Firearms (Sapp), 10

O
Obama, Barack, 15–16, 96–97
obscenity, 82
Office for Diversity, Literacy, and Outreach Services and the Gay, Lesbian, Bisexual, and Transgender Round Table (GLBTRT), 5
Office for Intellectual Freedom (OIF)
  Angela Maycock of, x
  censorship reporting, professional support for, 95–96
  censorship reports, scope of, 91–92
  databases, complaints about, 78
  Kristin Pekoll's work at, xi, xvi
  library displays, censorship of, 4–6
  reporting challenges to, 89
  silent censorship and, 94–95
"open, public forum," 36
opinion, 129
Oregon Association of School Librarians, 49–50

Oregon Battle of the Books (OBOB), 49–50
Oregon Intellectual Freedom Clearinghouse, 94
origin, 107, 118
Osefo, Wendy O., 66
Overdrive, 79, 86

P
Pacific Beach Library, California, 14
Packingham v. North Carolina, 68–69, 74
paper bookmarks, 46
Paper Girls (Vaughan), 3
"Paradise is Paper, Vellum, and Dust" (Macintyre), 29
parents
    access to digital resources and, 103
    censorship of library programs/events, 32–33
    censorship of reading lists, 49–50, 51
    databases, challenges of, 78–81, 86
    reconsideration policies and, 84
Parents' Rights in Education, 49
Parker, Alissa, 9
Parkland, Florida shooting, 9–10
Paste Magazine, 35
Pedagogy of the Oppressed (Freire), 53
Pekoll, Kristin, ix–xii
performing arts, 132–134
periodicals
    See databases
The Perks of Being a Wallflower (Chbosky), x, 48
"Perspectives on Islam" event, 31
Peters, Cal, 16
Peters, Robert L., 1
Peterson, Bob, 52–53
Picoult, Jodi, 9
Pima County, Arizona, 71
pipeline, 58–59
poetry, 25–26
police
    See law enforcement
policy
    for access to digital resources, 103
    for art display, 21–24
    for banning/restricting access to materials, 90
    for challenged resources, 109–111
    for databases, 83
    for exhibit spaces, 7–9, 120–121
    for library displays, 10
    for library programs, 39–41, 123
    for library space for visual/performing arts, 133–134
    reconsideration policies, 84–85

    for social media, 69–73
politics, 22, 64–65
pornography
    on databases, 78–81
    databases, challenges about, 86
    right to reference and, 81–82
post, right to, 67–69
posters, 14, 46
Postmaster General, Lamont v., 20
Poudre River Public Library District, Colorado, 14
preservation, 103
privacy
    in *Code of Ethics* (ALA), 137
    right to personal privacy, 129–131
    users' right of, 102
procedure
    for artwork, 24–25
    in program policy, 39–40
    for visual arts program, 24–25
professional support, 95–97
programming, 30
programming librarians
    creativity/passion of, 30
    supporting, 38–40
programs/events
    bias *vs.* balance, 40–41
    censorship of, 30–35
    as essential service for everyone, 29–30
    intellectual freedom and, 113
    "Library-Initiated Programs as a Resource" (ALA), 122–124
    programming librarians, supporting, 38–40
    right to speak/right to program, 36–38
    for visual/performing arts, 133
ProPublica, 69
ProQuest, 79
public agencies, 66–67
public forum, 36–38
public library, 91–92
Public Library Association, 30
Public Library of Cincinnati and Hamilton County, Ohio, 39
Pulphus, David, 16–17

R
racism
    banned books in Tucson, Arizona, 52–54
    censorship of art displays and, 16–18
    undocumented residents and, 34
Randall, Phyllis J., 66–67, 69
Ray-Saulis, Katrina, 6
READ poster, 15–16
readers' advisory, 45–46
    See also reading lists

Readers' Guide to Periodical Literature (database), 78
reading lists
  censorship/criticism of, 47–54
  direct/indirect means, 46–47
  pipeline, consequences of, 58–59
  professional freedoms, 55–57
  readers' advisory, 45–46
  right to suggest, engage, teach, 54–55
  values of academic freedom, 57–58
reconsideration
  of databases, 83
  policies, 84–85
  social media guidelines on, 73–74
reference, right to, 81–82
religion
  censorship of library programs, 31
  right to freedom of, 129
reporting
  of censorship, 89–90
  censorship data, 93
  scope of reports, 91–92
  selector vs. censor, 90–91
  silent censorship, 94–95
  support for, 95–97
"Request for Reconsideration" policy, 84–85
research, 77–78
resources, 63
  See also appendices; digital resources
Rethinking Columbus (Bigelow & Peterson), 52–53
Richmond, Virginia, 80
rights
  access rights of users, 102
  right to paint, 19–21
  right to post/right to block, 67–69
  right to reference, 81–82
  right to showcase, 6–7
  right to speak/right to program, 36–38
  right to suggest, engage, teach, 54–55
  right to use library, 124
  Universal Declaration of Human Rights, 112–113
  "The Universal Right to Free Expression" (ALA), 128–131
Rivonia Primary School, Johannesburg, South Africa, 67
Rogers, Mr., 4
Rolfe, Jo, 13
Rosales, Arturo, 52, 53
Rosier, Don, 64–65
Ross, Dennis, 33
Rossmann, Doralyn, 63
Rountree, Melissa, 19
Rudolph, Dana, 6
Rumford Public Library, Maine, 6, 7
Ryan, Paul, 17

S

Saga (Vaughan), 3
Saint Louis University, 8
Salt Lake County, Utah, 62
Santa Rosa County, Florida, 51
Sapp, Rick, 10
Saricks, Joyce, 45
school shootings, 9–10
School Shootings: What Every Parent and Educator Needs to Know to Protect Our Children (Lieberman), 9
selection
  criteria for reading list, 47
  decision to ban/restrict materials, 90
  selector vs. censor, 90–91
"Selection and Reconsideration Policy Toolkit for Public, School and Academic Libraries" (ALA), 84
selector, 90–91
sensor, 90–91
sexuality/sexual orientation
  "Access to Library Resources and Services Regardless of Sex, Gender Identity, Gender Expression, or Sexual Orientation" (ALA), 106–108
  censorship of programs/events, 30–33, 35
  databases, pornography on, 78–81
  reading lists, censorship of, 47–50
  See also LGBTQ
shelf talkers, 46
showcase, right to, 6–7
Siefker, Kayla, 80
Singular, Stephen, 10
Smithfield High School, Virginia, 80
Snyder v. Board of Trustees of University of Illinois, 37
social justice, xiii–xiv
social media
  censorship of, 64–67
  challenges via, 89–90
  for community communication, 61–64
  database challenges via, 82–83
  policies for, 70–73
  right to post/right to block, 67–69
  single voice, power of, 74
  "Social Media Guidelines for Public and Academic Libraries," 73–74
  social media managers, protection of, 69–70
  training for, 73
Social Media Curation (Valenza), 63

Index | 149

Social Media for Academics: A Practical Guide (Neal), 63
Social Media for Creative Libraries (Bradley), 63
"Social Media Guidelines for Public and Academic Libraries" (ALA), 73–74
social media managers, 69–70
Social Media Optimization: Principles for Building and Engaging Community (Young & Rossmann), 63
Solomon, Laura, 63
Sour Lake, Texas, 31–32
Southern Poverty Law Center, 86
speech
    See free speech
The Spiral Notebook: The Aurora Theater Shooter and the Epidemic of Mass Violence Committed by American Youth (Singular), 10
State Library of Louisiana, 51–52
Stonewall Award, 32
Stonewall riots, 5
Stranger Things (Houser), 3
Strasser, Todd, 9
Stripling, Barbara, 55
subject content, 3
subscribers, 82–86
Successful Social Networking in Public Libraries (Crawford), 63
Sullivan, New York Times Co. v., 125
support, 95–97
Surviving Columbine: How Faith Helps Us Find Peace When Tragedy Strikes (Carlston), 10

T
Taibbi, Matt, 35
Tampa-Hillsborough County Public Library, Florida, 6
technology, 46
Telecommunications Act of 1996, 67
Temple Public Library, Texas, 4–5
Texas ACLU, 94
The Third of May 1808 (Goya), 17
Thomas More Society, 80–81
Thomsett-Scott, Beth C., 63
tolerance, 4
Topeka, Kansas, 19
Torque Sequence (Itatani), 14
"traditional" public forum, 36
training, 69–70, 73
"Truman and Israel" event, 33
Truman Library Institute, 33
Tucson Unified School District, Arizona, 52–54

Twitter, 62, 64–65
Tyree, Michael, xi–xii

U
UEN (Utah Education Network), 79–80
United Nations, 112–113, 128–129
Universal Declaration of Human Rights, 112–113, 128–129
University of Kansas Medical Center's Dykes Library, 19
University of Missouri's School of Journalism, 94
University of Wisconsin, 16
unknown, xiii
U.S. Constitution
    artwork, protections for, 19–21
    censorship reports and, 91, 92
    internet filtering and, 104
    politics in libraries and, 125–126
    right to reference, 81–82
    right to showcase, 6–7
    right to speak/right to program, 36–38
    right to suggest, engage, teach, 54–55
    social media, right to post/right to block, 67–69
    See also First Amendment
U.S. Immigration and Customs Enforcement (ICE), 34
U.S. Supreme Court
    on challenged resources, 110
    on Fairness Doctrine, 68
    Miller v. California, 82
    Packingham v. North Carolina, 74
    on right to speak/hear, 37–38
users
    access rights of, 102
    access to library resources/services, 106–107
    library-initiated programs for, 122–124
    rights to use library, 118
    social media for communication with, 61–64
Using Social Media to Build Library Communities: A LITA Guide (Young & Rossmann), 63
Utah Education Network (UEN), 79–80
Utah Educational Library Media Association, 80
Utah Library Association, 80

V
Valenza, Joyce, 63
values
    design/culture and, 1
    equity, diversity, inclusion and, 115

values *(cont'd)*
  selector looks for, 90
Vaughan, Brian K., 3
viewpoints
  access to multiple viewpoints, 113
  collection diversity for multiple, 116
  inclusion principle and, 118
  library exhibits and, 120
  politics in libraries and, 125–126
Virginia Pharmacy v. Virginia Consumer Council, 7
"Visual and Performing Arts in Libraries" (ALA), 21–22
visual arts
  right to showcase, 6–7
  "Visual and Performing Arts in Libraries" (ALA), 132–134
  See also art
visual merchandising, 2
voice, 74

W
Walker, Kara, 18
walls, xiii–xiv

Washington, D. C., 16–17
Weather Underground, 34
website, library, 46
Webster's Dictionary, 30
Weeks, Jason, 51
Weeks, Linton, 45
Wells Public Library, Maine, 41
West Bend City Council, 49
West Bend Community Memorial Library, Wisconsin, ix–xii, 47–49
Whaley, John Corey, 52
Where Things Come Back (Whaley), 52
White, Molly, 5
Wise, Lisa, 32–33
Woolfolk, Steve, 33
Wyrosdick, Tim, 51

Y
Young, Scott. W. H., 63
YouTube, 62

Z
Zaragosa Escort Services, 79
Z.J. Loussac Public Library, Anchorage, Alaska, 5–6